INFAMY

Political Crimes and Their Consequences

Steven Greffenius

The Jeffersonian

Westwood, Massachusetts

For victims of 9/11, and their families

Contents

Part One:

November 22

Introduction: The First Conspiracy Theorist

Was Bobby Kennedy in on the plot to kill JFK? Before you think, good God, another nut, another preposterous theory, stay with me for this thought experiment. Consider these arguments. Bobby Kennedy had the means, motive, and opportunity to kill his brother. He had all the right connections with the Cuban exiles, trained in murder, ruthless and motivated to see the president dead. Fratricide was his surest path to the throne, once he put Lyndon Johnson out of the way. Jack trusted Bobby more than he trusted anyone else, and would never have guarded himself from his best friend.

The further you pursue this possibility, the more it makes sense. Yet no investigator, not even LBJ, thought of this possibility. When police gather evidence about a murder, the first people they question are those the victim knows best. Yet no one interrogated the president's brother. Instead of following standard procedure, the FBI fixed on Lee Oswald immediately after Kennedy died. It did not check in with the president's closest confidante at all. If the FBI had at least talked to the attorney general, they might have learned some interesting things.

Bobby Kennedy as the prime mover behind his brother's death resolves multiple mysteries connected with the event. Bobby was his brother's liaison with the CIA. Lee Oswald worked for the agency, and for the FBI, long before his employers set him up to take the fall on November 22, 1963. Second, the attorney general prosecuted Carlos Marcello, Mafia boss in New Orleans: Bobby Kennedy had him deported, in fact. Marcello had close ties with Jack Ruby, Oswald's killer, and plenty of reason to hate the Kennedys. Lastly, Bobby Kennedy failed to warn his brother about trouble in New Orleans, or threats that awaited him in Dallas. "I thought they would come after us," he said of his enemies when he heard the news from Texas, "but I thought it would be me."

Was that a clever instance of misdirection, to throw the FBI off the scent?

Most telling of all, Bobby Kennedy, despite his power as attorney general, never acted to find his brother's killer, or to discredit those who ginned up a false brief against Oswald. He permitted Lyndon Johnson and J. Edgar Hoover to concoct an incredible story about an inconsequential, low-level CIA operative firing on the president for no reason: with no motive at all that anyone could see. Bobby's friends were perplexed, because Bobby knew it could not be true. Yet he permitted the new president, the director of the FBI, and the chief justice of the Supreme Court pass off this nonsense to the public in a formal report. Bobby was the chief law enforcement officer in the country for most of the time the Warren Commission conducted its investigation. He could have done something to find the truth. Why didn't he?

Let's pause in this thought experiment for a moment. Do these arguments appear plausible? Perhaps. If nothing else, they show how quickly speculation about infamous, unsolved crimes can lead researchers into tricky terrain. No amount of formal, or even informal logic can overcome these difficulties. Evidence-based analysis and sound logic can resolve a lot of questions, but you can still make mistakes if you are not careful. That is one reason collaborative research produces reliable results: it prevents mistakes.

After I published this line of reasoning – dashed it off without identifying it as a thought experiment – a friend wrote to say, "I think you are completely off base on this one. ...Bobby did not pursue the real killers – LBJ and Allen Dulles and etc – because he needed the power of the presidency behind him to pull off the level of house cleaning required." With that I thought: time to do some analysis.

The first point concerns the opening question: "Was Bobby Kennedy in on the plot to kill JFK?" *In on* is not particularly useful for analysis or evaluation of evidence. It simply serves as a conversation starter if you want to play the *who dunnit* parlor game. It is entirely too open and imprecise. Was the Mossad *in on* the plot to blow up the World Trade Center? Was the Mafia *in on* the plot to kill Kennedy? Was the CIA *in on* the plot to kill Bobby Kennedy? These questions may be useful if they start one thinking, but they are weak tools for analysis or investigation. Researchers who want to draw defensible conclusions recognize the indeterminacy of a phrase like that. They refine weak questions, because weak questions yield weak results.

A second point of the thought experiment is to demonstrate, in a crime like Kennedy's murder, how you can make the implausible sound possible and even reasonable without doing much violence to well accepted knowledge. Tailor your sentences correctly, and you can create verbal illusions. The illusions become especially effective if you convince yourself they are true. Arlen Specter's magic bullet theory fits that description. Just as no one who has looked at the evidence believes the magic bullet theory, no one familiar with Bobby Kennedy thinks he had his brother murdered. Yet you can make the hypothesis appear reasonable enough. If that's the case, how do we reject or lay aside erroneous ideas and unsound logic in explanations of a complicated crime?

Inadequacy of the means, motive, and opportunity test

We know the means, motive, and opportunity test. A person who has the means, motive, and opportunity to commit the crime is a suspect. You often see this standard applied with the cui bono test, who benefits from the crime? As the Bobby Kennedy thought experiment suggests, both tests are of questionable value if not accompanied by other evidence. Yes, researchers can use these questions to rule suspects in or out, but the potential number of false positives is huge. That is, you include an enormous number of people in your suspect pool that could not possibly have committed the crime. Bobby Kennedy as a suspect in his brother's murder is an example. He meets the standard criteria for a suspect, but any investigator interested in the truth would know Bobby Kennedy is not a suspect.

Lee Oswald is another false positive, for that matter, though careful researchers would argue that he did not have an adequate weapon, a clear reason, or a clear shot. He certainly did not have a clear shot from Kennedy's right side, the origin of the fatal shot, because he was not located there. If we apply standard tests, one set of investigators might rule Oswald in and identify him as the sole shooter, as the Warren Commission did. Another set of investigators might use the same tests rule him out. Results of the means, motive, and opportunity tests are not unambiguous.

In sum, the three-part test seems rigorous, but it performs poorly when you want to rule people out. So you pretend to be rigorous when you are not. You think that if you make each suspect meet each test, you can eliminate all but a narrowly defined group. Every time you take another look, though, the number of people who had the means, motive, and opportunity expands still more. Bobby Kennedy becomes a prime suspect with this test, as do a host of Mafia figures and other assassins at the CIA's disposal. However you conduct your investigation, you cannot stop with the standard criteria.

Innuendo and non-sequiturs suggest false possibilities

The middle of the thought experiment teems with innuendo and non-sequiturs. If you think Bobby neglected his brother's welfare, you have travelled a long way down the wrong road. Yet liars in high positions can make anything sound reasonable. The idea that Bobby Kennedy killed his brother is no more improbable or outlandish than the idea that Lee Oswald did. The only reason people think Oswald killed the president is that someone with a badge, and someone named Earl Warren told them so. If the chief justice of the Supreme Court had reported that Elmer Fudd had assassinated the president, do you suppose anyone would have laughed at him? The lies put out before the United States attacked Iraq in 2003 show outlandish falsehoods accepted as true because people with weighty reputations gave the lies credence.

Lyndon Johnson was perhaps the most practiced liar of his generation, yet people did not recognize it till the debacle in Vietnam. Most people he led accepted his version of events in Dealey Plaza, where he ducked down in his car well before the first shots hit the motorcade. He knew what was coming, and he did not even have the manliness to sit up during the execution. Then he used his prestige, his personality, and his power to make fictional statements about the execution seem real.

Reasoning from negatives: why did something not happen?

The thought experiment asks why Bobby Kennedy, at the head of the Department of Justice, did not move to find his brother's killer. Reasoning from negatives can actually be a powerful tool. For the 9/11 attacks, one asks why the United States air defense system did not scramble fighters to intercept the hijacked airliners. When you use this type of reasoning, however, researchers have to compare what did happen with what did not. Government agencies and officials are well known for incompetence, neglect, mixed motives, poor judgment, bad decisions under pressure: all kinds of mistakes people are subject to. These weaknesses can cause people not to do things you might expect them to do. No matter how you consider the 9/11 attacks, inaction in that instance was so systemic that failure to respond to the attacks is inexplicable unless you assume a stand down order was in place.

In Bobby Kennedy's case, you needn't allow for mistakes or stand down orders. He was incapacitated by grief over the loss of his brother during the period that Hoover and his FBI collaborated with the Warren Commission to compile the commission's report. He was not an active attorney general during these months, nor was he in a position to be, given the rock-bottom state of his working relationships with Hoover and Johnson. After the Warren Commission's report came out in September 1964, the attorney general recognized that he could not pursue his brother's killers if he were not president. He had to know as well that if he was correct about who killed his brother, he would probably never become president.

David Talbot, in *Brothers*, writes that Bobby Kennedy was the first conspiracy theorist. The very day of his brother's murder, he suspected something. One hour after receiving confirmation of his brother's death, Bobby Kennedy confided to aide Edwin Guthman, "I thought they would get one of us. I thought it would be me." His suspicion would not subside during the months of grief that followed. Colleagues, family and friends asked him why he didn't follow up on his intuition. After all, he was still the attorney general. If he would lead an investigation, he would be doing right by his brother, right by the people who supported his brother, and right by his country.

Bobby replied, "What good would it do? It won't bring my brother back." Talbot also notes that Bobby could not have led an investigation even if he had wanted to. He was entirely isolated in the new administration. Lyndon Johnson and J. Edgar Hoover hated him. Johnson wanted him gone, but it would not look good to fire the assassinated president's brother. Bobby Kennedy could have poked around a bit as a private citizen, but he was not a private citizen. When he left the Johnson administration and became a private citizen, he did poke around a bit, but that was all.

I read once that Bobby showed extraordinary courage when he decided to run for president in 1968. He made his decision shortly before Johnson withdrew from the race. It took some political backbone to take on a sitting president. The courage in question, though, was not political but moral and personal. Bobby knew that if he was correct about a conspiracy to kill his brother in 1963, the same thing could happen to him in 1968, or shortly after. As soon as it looked like he might become president, he would become a dangerous person for the people who killed Jack. He won the California primary on June 4, 1968, and he was gunned down shortly after midnight the same evening. Some timing.

Can our country – all of us as citizens – demonstrate similar courage? Some people don't think we lost our republic on November 22, 1963. They think Oswald did it and we have to move on. Others believe the murder amounted to a coup d'état, but echo Bobby's initial, hopeless response to the idea that we ought to do something about it: "What good would it do? It won't bring our republic back." Others believe our republic began to slip away in 1963, and want to rectify the effects of this crime. That was Bobby's attitude in 1968.

The problem with this attitude, of course, is that we as citizens face the same consequences Bobby faced. Government has the capacity to kill us. It has the capacity to imprison us, to confine us to small cells twenty-three hours a day. It constantly demonstrates its willingness to use powerful instruments of intimidation and cruelty to protect its power and keep citizens quiescent. If you want to resist our government, as Edward Snowden has, you have to have the courage of Bobby Kennedy. You have to be willing to give your life.

When a Patriot Becomes a Patsy

The Jason Bourne thrillers have a lot of plot elements that pull you in: amnesia and discovery of one's identity, close calls and exciting escapes. One of the more compelling narrative lines is Jason Bourne's success as David against the government's gargantuan criminal enterprise: CIA's Goliath. He starts out as a patriot, and ends in a simple fight for survival. He foils all of his employer's efforts to kill him.

Real life for Lee Oswald did not follow the Jason Bourne narrative. Goliath in Washington crushed David in Dallas on November 24, 1963. Part of the difference was that Oswald did not have amnesia, so he was unwilling to leave his young daughters to go underground. Nevertheless, Oswald knew what was coming.

Lee's mother, Marguerite Oswald, declared – improbably at the time – that her son died in the service of his country. Even now that seems an incongruous thing to say, even if you know that Oswald was an agency asset set up to take the blame for the president's murder. The CIA was happy to have Oswald run a fake Fair Play for Cuba operation in New Orleans, even as Oswald and David Ferrie worked on a project to inject Fidel Castro with malignant cancer cells. Does that sound like another fantastic plot to come out of the CIA's Operation Mongoose? Do not discount it. Because of Oswald's low-level involvement with super-secret intelligence operations, he was the perfect patsy-villain for the operation that unfolded in six seconds of gunfire in Dealey Plaza on November 22.

The people who betrayed Oswald and made him a scapegoat knew their business. Scapegoats are vulnerable and ostracized: no one will speak for them at the time. They are completely alone, as Oswald assuredly knew when he pleaded for an attorney during his last forty-eight hours. Instead of letting him meet with an attorney, the Dallas police beat him.

As you learn about who Oswald was, the more you understand why he looks the way he does in photographs taken after his arrest on November 22, 1963. In particular, you come to understand the shape and expression of his lips, interpreted at the time as a smirk, along with the look in his eyes. You see a smart young man, a doomed scapegoat, coming to terms with the treachery practiced against him. He knows what's coming, yet he doesn't want to believe it.

Many argue, "If all those conspiracy theories were correct, someone would have talked. Where are they?" A simple answer is that people have talked. Often, people who know the truth suffer ostracism and even death, in the same way Oswald did. Judyth Vary Baker waited forty-five years to tell her story, and Lee's story. Baker had an affair with Lee in the summer of 1963. She worked with David Ferrie, Mary Sherman, and Lee Oswald in New Orleans during that summer. In a year, Oswald and Sherman would be dead. Ferrie would die early in 1967. Judyth Vary was the only one to survive. We are lucky she lived, for the memoir she published in 2008 tells a story no one else could tell. Her story explains Oswald's fate. It exonerates him, and shows how he found himself, in the middle of a November afternoon in Dallas, accused of murdering the president.

Vary's memoir, *Me and Lee*, sports what is supposed to be a tantalizing cover. Flip past the cover expeditiously. The cover shows little respect for the author: it suggests you are about to read a dime novel or second-rate romance, with the promise of sex in hot New Orleans. The memoir's content is entirely different. Vary explains, by virtue of her detailed account of Oswald and his work, why Oswald could not have been the president's assassin. She also explains how Oswald found himself in a position where the Dallas police and the FBI could accuse him of the murder.

By late July 1963, Oswald foresaw that he would be whacked, just as Ferrie and Sherman were in 1964. He did not know how or when it would happen, but he knew he was vulnerable as the Castro project reached an inconclusive point, and he worked through possibilities for the future. When he went to Mexico City for six days in September-October 1963, he must have considered whether he should try to disappear down there. He came back to be with his two daughters and estranged wife. On Wednesday evening, November 20, he has a poignant farewell conversation on the phone with Judyth Vary. She is in New Orleans, and he calls her from Dallas, she guesses from a phone booth. They talk for an hour and a half. He knows the president's trip to Dallas in two days likely means the end for him. He has already tried to warn the FBI about the plot against the president in Chicago earlier in the fall. Now he finds his handlers have placed him in the Texas School Book Depository.

Lee Oswald worked for both the CIA and the FBI through all of these eventful months, but he could not trust anyone in either of those organizations. When the Dallas police arrested him on Friday afternoon, November 22, the arrest did not come as a surprise. He cried, "This is it!" as police pulled him from his seat in the Texas Theater, where he went to lie low after the enormity in Dealey Plaza. He likely did not know that J. D. Tippit had been killed in the Oak Cliff section of Dallas. The route he took from Dealey Plaza to his room on North Beckley Street, and then to the Texas Theater on West Jefferson Boulevard, did not traverse the neighborhood on East 10th Street where Tippit died.

When you consider Oswald's experience during the forty-eight hours between his arrest on Friday and his murder on Sunday, November 24, you understand why he looked the way he did. Interrogated during the night and day, beaten about the face for no reason other than brutality and revenge, paraded in front of journalists and television cameras as the most hated man on the planet, friendless and without counsel, Oswald had to operate on his own. He suffered unbidden infamy without assistance. In this light, he does not look smug, and his apparent smirk looks not irritating, but prescient. He is a dismayed young man caught in a strong net, preparing himself for the worst. If the Dallas police had known he would stand up for himself, that he would volubly declare "I'm a patsy!" they may have been less ready to parade him around like a trophy. Nonetheless, they needed to parade him midday on Sunday, November 24, to give Jack Ruby a good shot.

Once you realize that Oswald worked for the CIA and FBI, and learn what he did for them, questions about Kennedy's assassination begin to resolve themselves. Vary's description of Oswald demonstrates what kind of person he was: energetic, intelligent, gracious and brave, savvy and competent. He was mature about the bad marriage he made in the Soviet Union, where he went for the CIA, and hopeful despite his poor prospects back in the States. Marguerite Oswald was right to point out that he was a patriot. He was not a Communist, a dangerous nut, a murderer, or a traitor. Right to the end, he did not reveal his work to anyone. He knew that without an attorney, his situation was as hopeless as it could be. Even so, he did not directly accuse his employers of betrayal. His declaration, "I'm a patsy," does suggest he grasped the significance of his arrest. He recognized his employers had something to do with Kennedy's death.

Warren Commission and Its Consequences

Exactly ten months after Jack Ruby shot Lee Oswald on national television, as Dallas police escorted Oswald out of their own jailhouse, the Warren Commission published its report on September 24, 1964. Fifty years later in September 2014, *Time* magazine congratulated itself on all the good work it did in 1964 to summarize the commission's findings for the nation. It actually expressed pride in the part it played to communicate key elements of the historic document. Here's an excerpt from the magazine's September 2014 article:

"We worked through the night and into a second night," recalls Marshall Loeb, now 85. "The mood was one of determination to get the story done."

In addition to recounting the events that surrounded the assassination, Loeb takes pride to remind us the Commission's report debunked the major conspiracy theories that had emerged in the year after that day: 1) Lee Harvey Oswald acted alone; 2) Lee Oswald and Jack Ruby had no connection; 3) there was foreign conspiracy, nor was there a domestic one.

If the Commission's report lacked scandal, Loeb continues, it provided detail. "Its great value comes from the thoroughness with which the Commission carried out its investigation, from its laying to rest many malignant rumors and speculations, and from its fascinating wealth of detail by which future historians can abide," he notes in *Time*'s story on the report.

One may as well say that *Time*, along with its sister publication *Life* magazine, helped perpetate an historic fraud. That's not something publishing organizations generally take pride in. Yet *Time* is steadfast. Time stands still. Fifty years after the event, the magazine still believes Lee Oswald acted alone. Jack Ruby did not know him. No conspiracy existed. To stand by these statements, given what we know now, makes you wonder what *Time*'s editorial staff has been doing the last fifty years. Can they possibly believe their readers regard the Warren Commission report now the way they saw it in 1964?

For many people, on the fiftieth anniversary, the Warren Report stands completely discredited. It stands as a symbol and enabler of treachery, a landmark of national betrayal, all the more egregious because the Supreme Court appeared to sanction it. The report did not reach this status because a bunch of nuts somehow persuaded people they had rational arguments and criticisms to make. The report is discredited by rational people who did careful work. To pretend that this work does not exist, as *Time* does, shows not only ignorance about the work itself, but an amazing blind spot about the impact this research has had on the way people think about the crime. You might call it Rip Van Winkle journalism. *Time* acts as if fifty years of investigation into why Kennedy died do not exist.

People say they no longer trust mainstream media. *Time* magazine's self-congratulations shows you why.

We like anniversaries partly because they make us pause to reflect. One reflection here reminds how you can reverse a lifetime of respected and distinguished work with one mistake. People recognized the quality of Earl Warren's work as a jurist, and as a politician, even if they disagreed with his liberal politics on the Court. Partly because of his reputation for integrity, he became Chief Justice of the Supreme Court. The same reputation led President Johnson to ask him to lead the commission that would investigate Kennedy's murder.

Johnson pressured Warren to take the job. He used the imperative that the Soviets would attack with nuclear weapons if this presidential commission did not investigate the crime, and calm people's fears of an international communist conspiracy. Warren might have responded, "If you think the Soviets will make a decision about nuclear war based on whether I take this assignment, you are not qualified for this office." He might also have said, "You want me to believe, Mr. President, that the Soviets will attack us with nuclear weapons if I don't lend my name to this commission? Where in your mendacious, manipulative mind does that kind of reasoning originate? What happens if the commission finds you and Hoover lied about who carried out this crime? What do you think the Soviets will do then?"

So Johnson forced the assignment on Warren under threat of nuclear war, a threat not connected with the assassination at all. People knew that Johnson deployed these gross falsehoods at will, that he would say anything necessary to get what he wanted. Warren must have known Johnson's affinity for lying, yet he accepted the job. Having done so, he should have continued to build his reputation for integrity, by finding the truth. Instead, Warren gave Johnson a bravely ingratiating, apparently thorough investigation dressed up to look like the truth. He assured thereby that his name, along with Johnson's and Hoover's, would become entwined with the coup that had just occurred.

Not long before the Warren Report came out in September 1964, FBI Director J. Edgar Hoover remarked over lunch to Bill Byars, Jr., son of a Texas oilman: "If I told you what I really know, it would be very dangerous to the country. Our whole political system could be disrupted." He made the remark about the FBI's investigation of John F. Kennedy's murder. Even the FBI director could not keep the secret to himself.

The Warren Report had not come out yet, but Hoover knew what would be in it. He knew the report would not disrupt the political system or be dangerous to the country. The purpose of the report, from the start, had been to reassure the country. Police had caught the assassin. Jack Ruby executed him two days later. Justice was done. The Warren Commission aimed to demonstrate the truth of this story, and to place the prestige of the nation's chief Supreme Court justice behind it.

Hoover knew the Commission's conclusions in advance, since the Federal Bureau of Investigation served as the primary – indeed the only – investigative resource available to the Warren Commission's staff. The staff could interview people on their own, but beyond that they had to rely on the FBI. As Hoover and his people conducted the investigation, they knew what conclusions President Johnson wanted them to reach.

Who besides a powerful person or a guilty person – with something to hide – thinks secrecy and dishonesty are less disruptive than the truth? Without a doubt, the truth disrupts. Dishonesty lets traitors and criminals cruise along on smooth water, as if their misdeeds had never occurred. The truth appears dangerous only to people who want to conceal their acts. Efforts to uncover criminal acts do not appear dangerous to the innocent, though the heavens may fall on the perpetrators.

When people began to reconsider Kennedy's assassination – who did it, how they accomplished it, and why – implicit fear about the country's safety lent an air of caution to the entire enterprise. "Don't go there," is the phrase we would use now. People apprehended then and later that the truth about Kennedy's death might have unpredictable consequences for our republic. Yet dishonesty is never the best policy. We can see, fifty years later, that the consequences of dishonesty during that period were substantially worse than anything the truth might have brought. The government might sail along on the ocean of falsehood in the Warren Report, but the country did not.

People said our nation lost its innocence on November 22, but that had already occurred before the fateful Friday afternoon gunshots. Kennedy would not have been murdered had the country been innocent. Most significantly, the country executed a decisive turn away from democracy both before and after Kennedy died. It did not recover than, and the consequences persist now. However hard the truth about Dallas might be, consequences that flow from the conspiracy to hide the truth have proven much worse. With the truth, we had a chance to save our republic. Without it – well, we know what happened without it.

No great power has, through crime and corruption, thrown away its position of civilizational leadership with such eager folly and utter ignorance. In the aftermath of Kennedy's murder, what would be "very dangerous to the country" justifies endless official measures of self-protection that serve criminals in power, not the people in the Constitution's preamble. We have seen the potential for falsehood to pollute the country's ideals, disrupt its institutions, and destroy its democracy. We have witnessed a lie so consequential, so potent that its effects corrupt everything government undertakes. No matter how dangerous the truth appears, lies are more dangerous still.

Texan Redemption

We've seen cracks form in the Union's foundation over the last several years. About half the states oppose the Affordable Care Act. About half the states have active secessionist movements. Some of these movements extend to the state legislatures. The states in the Southwest face a range of border issues that keep them generally unhappy with Washington.

Most of all, citizens have for decades now seen a large portion of their wealth transferred to incompetent government authorities who skirt the law. In fact, as the NSA disclosures show, they break the law at will. As HealthCare.gov and other ACA-related activities show, they cannot execute even visible, top-priority policies. As the IRS scandals show, they are willing to use the tax code to suppress First Amendment rights of free speech. The digest of ineptness, arrogance, dishonesty and malfeasance makes people ask, "What am I paying for here?"

States are the only power centers in our country that can effectively, persistently resist a federal government that has proven itself ineffective and out of control. Texas, for reasons of history, political culture, and geography is in the best position to lead this effort. It has one lever in particular that would seriously disrupt the states' relationship with Washington: the Kennedy assassination. To reopen this crime now would be like saying, "I'm going to reveal the family secrets, and here's why." Make the people who planned, executed, and investigated Kennedy's murder pay, posthumously, for their crimes and other misdeeds. J. Edgar Hoover once said, in private, "If people knew the truth about the Kennedy assassination, it would be very bad for the country." Let it happen. What is happening now is not worse.

If Texas takes the lead here, it has an opportunity to initiate a conflict where: (1) The outcome and consequences are unpredictable; (2) It holds a home field advantage; (3) Its opponent has no heart for the struggle, but has to enter the conflict nevertheless; (4) The conflict serves a purpose larger than the limited, legal aim of separation; (5) The state wins sympathy for its struggle from other states.

As the ostensibly weaker party in this conflict, Texas would benefit from all of these advantages. One might add that New York would enjoy similar advantages, were it to open a home field, locally focused investigation into the destruction of the World Trade Center.

To accomplish these aims, Texas should initiate a thorough investigation into the murder of John F. Kennedy in Dallas. Fifty years after the event, it should do what President Johnson prevented in 1963 and 1964. Forensic investigation immediately after the murder differs from historical research a half century later, but historical reconstruction has a few advantages. One of them is that Johnson is no longer alive.

We already know that the FBI, at Johnson's initiation, guided the investigation from Washington. Johnson moved to create a presidential commission a few days after Kennedy's burial. After that, Dallas officials and the Texas attorney general were largely out of the picture. Allen Dulles, on behalf of the Warren Commission, took responsibility for finding out who killed Kennedy. Despite all the effort his staff members put into their work, the responsibility was not so heavy. Life magazine and many other outlets pinned the murder on Lee Oswald as the sole killer long before Dulles's commission delivered its report. In fact, people believed they knew the killer's identity ninety minutes after the presidential limousine raced off to Parkland Hospital at 12:30 p.m. Johnson wanted the commission's imprimatur, not new information.

If the Texas attorney general reopened this case, Washington – the CIA and FBI in particular – would go nuts. Awkwardly, however, they could not appear to go nuts. Texas could force Washington into a conflict the feds do not want, yet the feds cannot walk away from it. To allow Texas officials a free hand in this case would yield far more truth than Washington could handle. We know how much the federal government depends on dishonesty in all its dealings to maintain its rule. We know that because it appeals so often to secrecy. Secrecy makes dishonesty possible. Dishonesty requires concealment. By contrast, transparent dealings force parties to conduct their relationships honestly.

For honesty's sake, Texas should pick this fight. Aside from the events that occurred in Dallas November 22, 1963, it should investigate related events before and after that date. Naturally it should concentrate on events that occurred in Texas, though we know New Orleans is next door. An investigation based in Texas can pick up the investigative threads that Jim Garrison developed during Clay Shaw's trial forty-five years ago.

The more locally based the investigation, the better. Texas investigators should not even look at the Warren Commission report. We already know what is in that study, and why it is there. Start fresh, the way a good historian would. Start with these general subjects: (1) What we know; (2) What we don't know; (3) What occurred in Texas before the murder; (4) What occurred in Texas the day of the murder; (5) What occurred in Texas after the murder.

The Texas attorney general should investigate how and why Kennedy died. He might also explain – for the historical record – what should have occurred in Texas after the murder, but did not. That explanation helps us understand the investigation Washington actually undertook in 1963 and 1964. Lastly, the attorney general should carefully select the person to lead the inquiry. A respected judge, who can assemble an impartial, skilled team would be a good choice.

Above all, the investigation should emphasize these specific areas, with a focus on events that occurred in Texas: (1) The planning and preparations that occurred before November 22; (2) Everything that happened the day of the murder, through the autopsy conducted during the early hours of November 23; (3) The so-called investigation conducted after the murder.

Everyone involved in this historical research – in Texas and in the rest of the country – knows its importance. Nearly everyone recognizes why. Key individuals in the federal government, including the attorney general, would act to stop the research. They could not ignore it, yet they would have no standing to block it. Texas should not back down: it should stoutly resist every attempt Washington makes to interfere with the research.

Who in Texas, a state with a lot of pride, would want to start a project that would reopen so sensitive a subject? Why risk the state's reputation now, fifty years later? Didn't the Dallas police already look incompetent when they let Jack Ruby shoot Lee Oswald? I would argue the opposite. This research could make Texas look better than any state has ever looked, in the whole history of the union. The truth in this matter is that important. Texas could pick a fight that determines not only its own future, but that of the whole country.

The city of Dallas might think its reputation will never recover, after it hosted President Kennedy, Kennedy's entourage, and Kennedy's assassins fifty years ago. Given the circumstances of JFK's murder, though, one shouldn't blame Dallas for the crime. Besides, cities don't commit murders: people do. Virulent, anti-Kennedy sentiments existed in central Texas in 1963, but people who cannot control their hate reside everywhere. Politicians, especially presidents, always attract their share of these dangerous, incomplete people. Virtually no one in Dallas wanted to see Kennedy killed. The people who planned and carried out his murder arrived from elsewhere.

Dallas law enforcement, however, bears a big load of responsibility for trying to conceal the truth about who murdered Kennedy, and about who murdered one of its own policemen, J.D. Tippit. In the days after November 22, Dallas police and prosecutors collaborated with the Federal Bureau of Investigation to hide the truth. Later, Dallas police realized the FBI consistently blamed them for various investigatory failures. By then it was too late: Dallas police couldn't get right with anyone. The Warren Commission published its report, to document the version of events cooked up ten months earlier among the FBI, Dallas law enforcement, and other interested parties. For the most part, the deception worked.

If Dallas wanted to redeem its reputation, it should not have launched the 50th anniversary Dallas Love Project. This idea amounts to kindergarten politics – adults commission kindergartners to broadcast sentimental sayings – sentiments with a barely disguised political motive – to make everyone feel better about their city. The plan, already underway, is to line Kennedy's motorcade route with posters about love. Honestly. Enter Dallas Love Project in Google Images to see Dallas's preferred response to the fiftieth anniversary of a president's death on the city's streets.

Is that how we recall our distinguished, courageous leader in our struggling republic? What a saccharine, misplaced idea, given the gruesome, grotesque execution that occurred in Dealey Plaza, near Houston and Elm. The idea that educators and other municipal leaders would enlist little five- and six-year-olds in this feel-good, futile cover-up is appalling. Underneath the watercolors, the construction paper, the Elmer's glue and the elementary school sweetness, the wound inflicted on all of us – and on Dallas – fifty years ago still works its harm.

If Dallas aims to repair its reputation five decades on, city leaders ought to: (1) Do what they can, with local resources and fifty years of history behind them, to uncover the truth about why Kennedy died; (2) Unearth the complicity of Dallas police and prosecutors in helping the feds lie about who committed the crime; (3) Insist that the feds come clean, too; (4) Lead the rest of the country to reconsider the evidence, to reject lies and accept the honest truth, and to accept what the truth implies; (5) Organize itself to resist federal interference with its activities, and to accept help for this resistance from other cities and states.

The people of Dallas, and of Texas, have the guts, resources and motivation to undertake a truth-telling project of this magnitude. The crime took place in Texas, and local knowledge counts for a lot. Most of all, Texas has the required spirit of independence. It has the rough edges and Sam Houston-like courage to gore Washington's detestable heart. The CIA, the FBI, the Warren Commission, the White House, the mainstream press, and any other federal body or federal affiliate involved in planning, executing, or covering up the assassination should come under scrutiny, to the extent that people in Dallas are able to press those questions.

Locally, the coming-clean investigation can start by endorsing the doctors at Parkland hospital, by backing up what they said about Kennedy's wounds. It can move from that significant step to the obvious: that Jack Ruby's killing of Lee Oswald was not a mistake. It might appear to show police incompetence, but what we truly need to know is the level of police complicity in the contract killing. Dallas's inquiry should leave no embarrassing or damning detail untouched. In particular, it should reexamine everything that happened both before and after the president's bloody Lincoln arrived at Parkland hospital's emergency entrance.

Texas has a political tradition of not giving a damn what the feds say. If the Lone Star State – Dallas especially – were to live up to that tradition now, during this season of remembrance, it could take a healing and even heroic step. The country would respond to Dallas's leadership and guts.

Instead, if city leaders choose to line Kennedy's motorcade route with bright paintings and happy sayings about love, we may as well finish our walk down Main Street with a trip to the Sixth Floor Museum, in the old Texas Schoolbook Depository. As its name suggests, that is the museum that spins the standard tale of how Kennedy died. How many people have stood near the site of Lee Oswald's presumed "sniper's nest," recreating in their minds an act he never committed? In that museum, you see and hear a story that brings shame to the city. In that museum, you see – in pictures and words – the lies that Dallas's authorities helped create.

John F. Kennedy and the Unspeakable

I lived in Nanjing, China when Oliver Stone's film, *JFK*, came out. We were cut off from a lot of news over in China. You felt like you were on the other side of the world because you were. So something had to make a big stir in the U. S. for us to know about it in Nanjing. The Los Angeles riots after police beat Rodney King and the first Persian Gulf war were two events that made a stir. Oliver Stone's film did, too.

I didn't see the film until much later, well after we returned to the United States. Before that I saw an interview where a journalist asked Stone whether he believed the story he told in JFK. He smiled slightly and said, "I just make movies." I thought it was a good answer. I didn't feel so comfortable if, after nearly thirty years of controversy, the judgment of so many people would turn on the story presented in one film.

After we returned from China, I read Gerald Posner's book, *Case Closed*. The controversy about Stone's film must have raised my interest, as it was the first book about the assassination I'd read. Posner's argument, that Lee Oswald acted alone and that a single bullet hit both President Kennedy and Governor Connally, seemed plausible. I hadn't been inclined to question the Warren Report to begin with, so Posner's account was convincing enough for me.

Now move forward ten years and more, to the Bush administration's response to 9/11. The regular use of torture by the CIA and the military against our enemies appalled me. It completely changed my attitude toward my own government. Where before I would give my elected representatives the benefit of the doubt in every doubtful case, now I would never do so. I completely lost faith that the government would do the right thing as it carried out its responsibilities. The government's behavior after 9/11 caused it to lose legitimacy.

Some would say, "It's about time you saw that." Others would say, "Governments have always done bad things. These acts weren't out of the ordinary. You have to take the bad with the good." A third bunch might comment simply, "Open your eyes and try not to be so idealistic." Open your eyes is right, but not in the way the last group intends. Remember Saul's conversion, when the scales fell from his eyes after God struck him blind? He was a new person after that. What a conversion experience – Paul went out and converted the world after that.

Let me describe my conversion experience. Mine started in 2002, when we started down the path toward war with Iraq. I've already written a lot about that period in Ugly War. Anger preceded Bush's reelection in 2004; discouragement followed it. By 2005, though, my emotion and vehemence had played out; the horrific events in Baghdad and elsewhere during Bush's second term made me feel beyond anger. As Bush's popularity bottomed out and stayed low during 2005-2007, I thought, I was here a long time before everyone else.

Then in the summer of 2009 I read an article by Oliver Stone in praise of a new book by James Douglass. Douglass's book is titled JFK and the Unspeakable: Why He Died and Why It Matters. I bought the book at Amazon, and as often happens at that site, picked up another book, too, called Brothers by David Talbot. I read Brothers first, and could see it was a first class piece of journalism. I said to people, if you're interested in the Kennedys, you have to read this book – and I don't recommend books that often. Then I started Douglass's book.

As I read Talbot's account, I found myself saying, "We'll never know if there was a conspiracy behind Kennedy's assassination." As I finish JFK and the Unspeakable, I ask, "How could anyone who considers the evidence think otherwise?" The main problem with Stone's film, and with Jim Garrison's work in the 1960s, is that they don't explicate a motive for a government conspiracy. You're left feeling that everyone was in on it. How could so many people be involved with the conspiracy, and still have it be a secret after all this time?

Well, the number of people involved, or who knew about the conspiracy, was large but not that large. As for secrecy, it's amazing how much evidence related to a conspiracy was ready at hand from the start. What a poorly kept secret! Yes, the Warren Report managed to corral enough people who would speak in favor of the lone gunman account of the crime. Its purpose from the start was to lay conspiracy theories to rest, and it succeeded with people like me – people brought up to give our public institutions more trust than they apparently deserve. After the Bush-Cheney fiasco, I would never ever misplace my public trust again.

Let me say a little about the word conspiracy before moving on to Douglass's book. The term has a bad odor after many years of dismissive put-downs: "Oh, he's just another one of those conspiracy theorists." Remember the simple meaning of conspiracy: it refers to a secret plan by a group to do something unlawful or harmful. Reduced further, it means more than one person was involved in the assassination. Was it a lone gunman or not? If you think it wasn't a lone gunman, do you have to live with the opprobrious label, conspiracy theorist?

The virtue of Douglass's book is that he explains why a conspiracy formed in the first place. It's the first book that convincingly addresses the conspirators' motives. In Case Closed, Posner recognizes that he has to accomplish the same tasks as a courtroom attorney: assemble evidence to support your case, explicate a motive, make the evidence and the motive hang together in a convincing story. Douglass makes the opposite case convincing because he tells a convincing story. You have to ask why it happened, and have a plausible answer. I haven't read all of the conspiracy literature, but I can tell you that an awful lot of it focuses on evidentiary details. Jim Garrison's case is a good example of that method. One reason the jury acquitted Clay Shaw is that Garrison didn't explain why Shaw might have been involved with a conspiracy to begin with.

When you read Talbot and Douglass together, you can see that many powerful people had numerous reasons for wanting Jack and Bobby Kennedy out of the way. At bottom, they saw Jack Kennedy as treasonous, not to be trusted with the power he held. Brutus and the other conspirators in Rome had the same motive for killing Caesar. They didn't trust him. They didn't trust him with the survival of the state. In Kennedy's case, his enemies believed that if he continued as president, the United States would lose its global contest with communism.

Imagine that Barack Obama wants to open negotiations with Osama bin Laden, early in his first term. When challenged, told firmly he should not go down that road, Obama persists. He argues that we invite our own destruction if we don't find a way to make peace with our enemies. He argues that we should look at our own attitudes, examine our own tendency to reach for weapons of war when the methods of peace offer us our only hope for salvation. The differences between our current war and the Cold War of Kennedy's time are numerous and relevant, yet this example gives an idea of the reaction some people had toward Kennedy's moves toward reconciliation with the Soviet Union after the Cuban missile crisis. Like Kennedy, they perceived the nation's survival at stake. They concluded that Kennedy must be removed from office to protect the republic.

When you understand the conspirators' motives, the rest of the evidence becomes too strong to dismiss. Douglass assembles a huge amount of non-dismissible evidence to support the conclusion that the CIA was involved in Kennedy's murder. For me, Jack Ruby's murder of Lee Oswald on November 24 created the small voice that asked through the decades, "What's going on here? That's fishy." How could Oswald be murdered like that? What's going on here?

Then you learn that Jack Ruby had ties to the CIA before he carried out his hit against Oswald. You learn that Oswald wasn't only a former Marine, a loner and a misfit with problems in his marriage and no steady job. His history was a lot more complicated than that. Life magazine published that black and white photograph of Oswald, standing with a rifle in his hands. There you have him, the president's killer. The evidence is right in front of you. When you find out that Oswald himself worked with the Central Intelligence Agency, had done so for quite a long time before 1963, you have to question the Life magazine account. You can't believe the Warren Report any longer when you learn that both Jack Ruby and Lee Oswald had clear ties to the CIA.

The enormity of the alternate account was too big for most people to swallow. How could our own government have been involved with this huge crime? The crime itself couldn't be believed. Political assassinations of the kind that brought Julius Caesar down just don't occur any more. Instinctive disbelief in political assassination engendered grief-stricken belief in the Life magazine account: a disturbed gunman acted alone, for reasons we could never fathom due to Jack Ruby's act of revenge.

Well what if Jack Ruby didn't act out of revenge? What if he cried that weekend not because Kennedy was dead, but because he'd been assigned to take Oswald out? He'd cry if he knew his life was over. He went to prison and died there. Oswald cried out to the press the day before, "I'm just a patsy!" Funny thing for a presidential assassin to say, actually. Funny thing to say if, as Posner argues, he shot Kennedy to make a name for himself. Funny thing to say, unless it's true.

So read Douglass's book. Read it even though it looks a little dense and intimidating. Good research generally looks that way. One Amazon reviewer commented that this book is the most important written in the last forty years. That is not an overstatement, no matter what you think of the Kennedys and no matter what you think of the Warren Commission. JFK and the Unspeakable offers our country an opportunity to deal with the truth. The country is already immeasurably weakened now, at the beginning of 2010, compared with its strength and vitality at the end of 1999. At the least, it can muster courage to recognize the truth before it passes into history's list of deflated and fallen empires.

J. K. Rowling said that dealing with the truth is always better than accepting a lie or an evasion. Not only better – it's easier than the alternatives, no matter how hard accepting the truth might be.

We don't know what might have happened in the United States if we had accepted the truth about November 22, 1963, right away. We do know what will happen if we don't accept it now. Our country will succumb to civil conflict, just as Rome did after Caesar fell. We had plenty of civil conflict in the 1960s, and we have plenty more on the horizon now.

Conspiracy theorists have another kind of dismissive put-down to deal with. "You think JFK's assassination was an inside job? So what if it was? What can we do about it? Let's move on already." Bobby Kennedy wasn't dismissive about it, but during his bitter period of grief in 1964 he said something similar. "What good would it do to prove a conspiracy? It won't bring my brother back." Who cares if people in our own government knocked off a sitting president? It happened over fifty years ago. Let's deal with problems we have right now.

Oliver Stone, David Talbot and James Douglass have it right, though. We can't pretend Kennedy fell to a lone nut if it's not true. We have to be clear eyed about why facing the truth matters. We have to face the enormity of this assassination. If it's the truth, we have to accept that our government executed a president, then lied to cover it up. How could anyone say that the truth doesn't matter here? We all want to love our country. We all want to be proud of our citizenship, our membership in a constitutional community for freedom and responsibility. How can love and pride ring true for us if the whole project rests on a lie that big?

Once you've lost faith in one area, you lose faith in every area. The government tortured people to death at Bagram air force base, and you wonder what else it can do. Once you doubt that Lee Oswald acted alone, you doubt that Sirhan Sirhan acted alone. Once you doubt the government's story about why the Kennedys died, you doubt the official story about Malcolm X and Martin Luther King. When you don't believe anything the government says, that's not healthy skepticism anymore. That's a loss of faith so complete the government no longer holds legitimate authority.

That's the corrosive consequence of betrayal. Once you doubt one act or statement, you doubt every act, every statement. Once you see that the government secretly, then openly runs torture camps – with a worldwide network it uses to transport prisoners to designated torture sites – you ask what else it does. I can't think of a policy that stoops lower than that. It was just the Holocaust with fewer people.

Loss of trust goes a long way: you distrust every last element of authority you used to deem legitimate. You used to pay taxes because you wanted to support public institutions, because you believed in their mission. You believe your representatives carry out their responsibilities openly and in good faith. You are proud of your membership in the community, and you believe in its purpose. Once you lose trust, you lose all those beliefs. Once you lose trust, you pay taxes because you have to, and your membership becomes a disgrace.

We know the 1960s weren't easy – Vietnam stretched most Americans' patriotism hard. I'm glad I didn't have to make a decision between fighting Viet Cong or resisting the draft board. I have deep admiration for soldiers like John Kerry who fought honorably, then opposed the war when they returned. That took courage. On the other side, the so-called patriots who swift-boated John Kerry are nothing more than professional liars and opportunists: people who will say and do anything – no matter how unethical – to get their candidate elected. It's especially galling that the beneficiary and tacit backer of the swift boat campaign, George W. Bush, sat out the war in his air national guard unit while Kerry and others led brave men into battle. Bush knew the swift boaters were lying, yet said nothing to defend Kerry's honorable service.

After Vietnam, I joined the Navy voluntarily, when the armed forces still lived under the ignominy of that misbegotten war. Service to country was a primary motive. My love of country survived Vietnam, but living through that time taught me that loving your country does not require loyalty to its government. You can maintain fidelity to your country's ideals while you stand against the actions of its government. The same distinction has to hold for patriots who recognize the evil behind our government's actions, whether those actions involve assassination or torture. Condemnation of the government for acts that are in fact evil is not disloyal, unpatriotic, or treasonous. Let the truth about evil come out, though the heavens – or government – may fall.

Would the heavens fall if we acknowledged the truth about JFK's assassination? Would they have fallen if we had acknowledged it fifty years ago? We can't answer the second question, of course. We can only answer the first question about what would happen now if we try it out. Sixteen years after the assassination, in 1979, the House panel on assassinations wrote that Kennedy's murder was probably the result of a conspiracy. After Oliver Stone's film, polls began to show more than half of American citizens believe the same thing. Does that mean we've acknowledged the truth? I don't think so. Acknowledging the truth means we open up all of our government's records on the matter. To begin with, those records belong to us. Acknowledging the truth means that our government take an active role in finding the truth, not an active role in concealing it. Acknowledging the truth means owning the crime, and figuring out where to go from here once we've done so.

I'd say we owe James Douglass a big debt of thanks. That book took a lot of work. It took special skill to do what he did. As citizens we need to read his work and reach judgments about what he has written. Honestly, you can't let your president be murdered and not face up to it. You can't let the unspeakable remain unspoken. At some point the unspeakable has to come into the open and enter the room, no matter what. When it does, you have to keep it with you, no matter how shocking, shameful, or shattering the truth is.

I'm telling you, we have one more chance, after George W. Bush, to save our country, to reestablish our commitment to its founding ideas and principles. We have big trials ahead. Acknowledging the truth about our government's crimes could help us survive the coming trials as one nation. If the country and its citizens hide the truth, avoid it and hope it disappears, we'll shatter into a shapeless pile under the pressures we'll endure. We don't have to endure these trials alone, we don't have to succumb, but the general atmosphere of division and pessimism suggests that we prefer failure to honesty.

Part Two:

September 11

Origins of the 9/11 Truth Movement

About a generation and a half elapsed between November 22, 1963, to September 11, 2001: thirty-seven years, nine months, and twenty days. If you were born the day Kennedy died, your children would be youngsters on 9/11, as I was on November 22, 1963. We let something terrible happen in 1963: criminals murdered our president, and we did not raise holy hell when they lied about what they had done. A little over thirty-seven years later, the institutional children of those criminals struck again, and we did the same thing. We let them get away with it.

After long, careful and thorough research, we have good evidence now that we permitted a coup in 1963. A long time passed – more than forty years – before many of us understood or believed that. We don't know yet what occurred on September 11, 2001. The events of that day present more complications than does delivery of a bullet to a leader's head. Complex or not, we do not have fifty years to grasp the significance of 9/11. To save our republic, we have to face what happened that day as soon as possible.

To undertake this project of understanding, we should recall that the desire to discover what happened on 9/11 does not originate with a group of extremists who see a government conspiracy behind every horrible event. Efforts to learn the truth about 9/11 originate with victims' families. Family members lost wives and husbands, sons and daughters, mothers and fathers, brothers and sisters. They lost the people they loved most without warning, in circumstances that called for explanation. These were not natural deaths: victims died at the scene of an enormous crime. When that happens, you want to know who murdered them. How and why the murderers committed the crime is also on your mind.

Each person in the towers walked into the front door of the building that sunny September morning, ready to work one more day. They took the elevator to the floor where they would meet their friends, sit at their desks, place phone calls, type messages to colleagues. Everything seemed like every other morning. Thirty minutes later, they are saying goodbye to their spouses on their cell phones, or standing at a shattered window to decide whether they ought to jump. Most of the people who died that morning had loved ones at home, in school, in cities nearby. Those family members had dinner that night with an empty space at the table, went to sleep that night with an empty space in the bed. They knew the empty space would not be filled again.

When something like that happens to your family, you want to know why. Your grief won't permit you to forget. You press for an investigation, but you find quickly enough that the officials you ask are too busy for you. They tell you politely, with well-practiced indirection, we have better things to do. They tell you to go away: we'll give you money if you go away. They tell you we already know everything we can find out. They tell you things you know cannot be true. You come to understand that they snow you and avoid you compulsively: they act under implicit orders to do so. You cannot trust them with even the simplest request or task.

The 9/11 truth movement began with family members who dealt with officials like that: dilatory officials who were dishonest, unforthcoming, deceptive, unresponsive and, in the end, unsympathetic. When the victims' families would not give up, the president chartered the 9/11 Commission more than fourteen months after the attacks. The Commission submitted its final report nearly three years after September 11, in 2004.

To show his level of support for the body he formed, the president would not speak with the Commission for the record. He did not give a reason. Anything he had to say would be privileged and private. If the president would not cooperate with the Commission, who else in the government would? The president's example told everyone in government to treat the Commission's inquiries the same way the officials had had treated inquiries from the victims' families. When people request classified information, you have to tell petitioners they cannot have it, without telling them why they cannot have it. You have to bury the information, to prevent it from becoming evidence against you.

Cass Sunstein, an earnest, unfortunate law professor who happened upon a position of responsibility serving this corps of organized criminals, calls people in the truth movement epistemological cripples. He suggests these cripples threaten us, because they spread falsehoods about their government. They are so dangerous and unbalanced, he claims, government law enforcement agencies should infiltrate these groups to destroy cohesion, spread rumors and lies, sow conflict, and disrupt their effectiveness.

That is how a government official responds to people who just want to know how their dad or their mom wound up buried under a thousand tons of rubble, with molten steel flowing around their bodies. Sunstein ridicules parents who reject lies and excuses, when they ask simple questions about why their sons and daughters died. He devises deceitful, aggressive strategies to derogate, discourage, demoralize and demean spouses who want to know, justifiably, what happened to their wives and husbands.

Today, the 9/11 truth movement represents men and women who just want to know the nature of these crimes, and who want justice. It does not represent extremists, nuts, anarchists, spies, violent troublemakers, or other misfits. Individuals who insist on the truth pose a threat only to those complicit. Information they want to publicize does not threaten, but enhances national security in the long run.

If revelation indicts institutions who guard this information and control it, so be it. In democracies, institutions exonerate themselves with openness and honesty. Everywhere else, public institutions conceal their guilty acts.

Independent Research About 9/11

Let's sum up quickly the current state of thinking among skeptics. They would agree on these general points: (1) evidence in hand demonstrates official accounts of 9/11 are false; (2) current evidence is insufficient to give a full account of what actually did happen on 9/11; (3) therefore, we need a new investigation. None of these points, not even the first, is particularly controversial. Become acquainted with David Ray Griffin's work, and you'll see why I say that. If government accounts had even half the integrity of Griffin's, Americans might give official spokesmen benefit of the doubt. As it is, no reasonable person can read Griffin's thorough work without concluding, "We have to find out what is going on here."

Read chapter ten in Griffin's *The New Pearl Harbor*, titled *The Need for a Full Investigation*. Read other chapters. You will think, "Griffin has a sure grasp of his logical and evidentiary tools, like a skilled attorney. I would not want to face this gentleman in a courtroom!" He handles evidence so well, so methodically and with such intelligence, that defenders of the official account appear careless, thoughtless, feckless or malicious – take your pick. By comparison with Griffin's own care and thoughtfulness, his subjects have neither intelligence nor skill to accomplish the fraud he uncovers. Accomplish it they do. They radiate easy self-assurance about their excuses and evasions. Their lies seem reasonable until Griffin suggests, "Let's have another look."

In Plato's dialogues, Socrates often makes his interlocutors look foolish. That's why they avoided him, and eventually condemned him. So it is with Griffin, though interestingly, people who dismiss conspiracy theories simply ignore him. He patiently analyzes official claims to show how weak, self-contradictory, and ultimately groundless they are. Griffin is a philosopher as well as a theologian, and his training shows. If you want to argue with him, you need to be well prepared.

Griffin does not go against only weak and unskilled opponents, either. Cass Sunstein is a capable legal philosopher out of the University of Chicago. In *Cognitive Infiltration*, Griffin makes Sunstein look foolish and unprepared: like a student who did not do his homework, as a matter of fact. To Griffin's credit, he does not send up Sunstein's claims and proposals to add a notch to his own record. Sunstein's arguments appear crude in light of Griffin's critique. They are also weak and ill-conceived. They deserve a rebuttal. I am curious how Sunstein felt when he read Griffin's book. Significantly, Sunstein chose not to respond to Griffin's critique in writing. Perhaps he knows how to cut his reputational losses.

Let's consider implications for skeptics' point three: their call for a new investigation. Griffin, architects and engineers who agree with him, and many others have advocated research that accounts for all evidence related to 9/11. That would include what happened before that day, an account of the day itself, as well as what happened after the towers and World Trade Center 7 fell. In short, they want an impartial examination of evidence that tries to uncover what actually happened on 9/11. How did nearly three thousand citizens die that day?

Here is advice from one 9/11 skeptic: find out who, and the how will follow. That is, find out who is responsible for the 9/11 crimes, and details about how the criminals destroyed the buildings will become clear. The difficulty is, evidence about who committed the crimes is the hardest to get. It is secret, and in the hands of people who will not give it up.

Griffin is clear as well about who should conduct the investigation: Congress or the press. The executive branch had its chance with the 9/11 Commission and failed. The Commission's report felt like its infamous predecessor, the Warren Commission report: inaccurate, incomplete, and insufficient. Even though the crime was far more complex than Kennedy's assassination, the 9/11 Commission report is much shorter. It does not even address the most glaring evidence of foul play, the destruction of World Trade Center 7. Like the Warren Commission report, it overlooks innumerable other pieces of evidence, all of them significant and in need of analysis.

Incredibly, George W. Bush resisted requests from victims' families for an inquiry for over a year and a half, as evidence grew cold, or was scattered and destroyed. When the Commission wheeled out the results of its work, people who had taken an independent look at the matter could not contain their criticism. One would want to snicker, if the crime were not so serious.

The 9/11 truth movement wants a report that does justice both to the evidence and to the truth. A board of inquiry appointed by Congress would have the independence, resources, skills, and motives to investigate 9/11 properly. In good faith, professional journalists would bring the same qualities to investigations they conduct. Either institution – or the two working along parallel tracks and in their own ways – could produce work superior to the report the 9/11 Commission produced.

The only people who can conduct valid research about 9/11 are independent researchers who have already undertaken it. They need encouragement, support, and new recruits to continue this essential work. Just as important, we ought to keep demanding that government release information about 9/11 that it guards so closely. Government officials know instinctively that their authority will evaporate if they resist these demands indefinitely. Meantime, independent researchers have to keep at their work. They are the only ones with integrity, skill, and motivation to succeed.

Truth Will Out

We have to consider for a few moments the stated aim of individuals in the 9/11 truth movement. When people challenge their evidence, their reasoning, their implied conclusions, their analytical methods, or other elements of their case, 9/11 skeptics say we need a new, impartial investigation. It is a reasonable aim, and a modest one. In its modesty, it deflects the challenges people would like to pose for the group.

A practical difficulty with this request is that movement leaders do not indicate who should conduct an impartial investigation. A qualified team of investigators would need resources, access to relevant information, and a variety of skills. They would need a charter of some sort to give their work direction and legitimacy. They would need to use methods of research that lend themselves to credible, defensible conclusions. Most of all, they would need to present their findings in a competent, reasonable manner.

With people like Cass Sunstein working for the White House, the battle lines in this conversation are already drawn. Many – we call it the main stream now – would regard new, better supported conclusions as incredible no matter what investigators find. In a partisan arena, where the legitimacy of our government is at stake, consider how an investigative team might produce results that would not be killed in the cradle, or – even worse in our political culture – simply ignored. Ridicule and disbelief are just two possibilities, oblivion is another.

Sponsorship and access to evidence

Given these considerations, ask who would sponsor such a group of investigators. The sponsoring organization would select the group's members, fund the group's investigation, and help the group achieve its goals. It would facilitate the group's activities, so the team could concentrate on research, organize and evaluate evidence, prepare summaries and reports, and assemble its results coherently. The sponsor could be inside of government, or outside of government. If inside, taxpayers would fund the investigation. If outside, money from private sources would fund the research, or volunteers would conduct the research gratis.

Whatever the source of funds, the group would need access to relevant evidence. Without access, it would have nothing to do. We have to establish this principle: when government withholds evidence about a crime, that is obstruction of justice. Our legal system treats obstruction of justice as a crime. When government tries to conceal evidence for a crime as enormous as 9/11, it should have to defend itself in an independent court against an accusation that it has obstructed justice. If government conceals evidence and nothing happens, why would the obstructers change their behavior?

To mount an independent investigation that originates within government would be a foolish, futile, and questionable enterprise. We already know from bad experience that government is untrustworthy. The 9/11 Commission already completed an investigation that is practically empty of answers to outstanding questions. Key agencies of government have no incentive or motivation to supply evidence required for an investigation. Why should we expect a new investigation conducted by government to improve the one it has already completed?

That leaves a privately sponsored investigation. Here the progress of research into the Kennedy assassination offers a good lesson. Efforts of private researchers over five decades revealed far more useful information about this event than the Warren Commission did in its twenty-six volumes. Pressure from private researchers, and from the public, gradually forced government agencies to make more documents available than they would have if left alone. The new evidence revealed since the Warren Commission report has made a difference. President Johnson's purpose in creating the Warren Commission was to close the books on this crime. In that key aim, he and the Commission failed.

Credit belongs to the persistence and perseverance of all the Kennedy researchers who worked without sponsorship, without pay, and without an official charter to give weight to their results. They suffered mockery, threats, ridicule, ostracism, and contempt, yet they stayed with their research. Some individuals, like Mary Meyer, died for their loyalty to the truth. Others lost their jobs, their friends, and their reputations.

Researchers into the Kennedy assassination patiently made their case until they left their opponents looking like the Black Knight in Monty Python and the Holy Grail. A decisive preponderance of evidence has sliced off every defense for Warren Commission apologists, yet lone nut theorists continue to sputter their challenges. They used to speak so confidently, even superciliously, as if their opponents were beneath notice. Now, as evidence for a conspiracy accumulates, they stand as defeated, slightly pitiful amateurs who cannot admit they were mistaken.

A new investigation of 9/11

As we think about prospects for a new investigation into 9/11, remember our government has become tyrannical and obsessive in its desire to protect information. Certainly it is more closed about information related to 9/11 than it has been about records related to the Kennedy assassination. If government sponsored investigators could not gain access to relevant evidence, the same barriers would hold for private researchers. Freedom of Information Act requests will not do here.

As with the Kennedy assassination, private researchers have to rely on their ingenuity, their resourcefulness, and their investigative skills to make progress. We know that 9/11 is a more complex event than the Kennedy assassination. The operation required more coordination than sending a team of assassins to kill one man. Moreover, 9/11 does not have a prominent piece of evidence like the Zapruder film or the Ruby-Oswald hit to serve as touchstones for other work. The destruction of World Trade Center 7 gives a critical foundation for research, but for many the event is not so prominent. The evidence about 9/11, like the operation, is more dispersed than for the Kennedy assassination.

No matter the difficulties, private groups and individuals will continue their work. Architects and Engineers for 9/11 Truth, for one good example, have assembled sound evidence and arguments related to events in New York at the World Trade Center on September 11. They have professional pride, patriotism, and a sense of conscientious citizenship to motivate their work. If what the government says about 9/11 is true, then architects and engineers who design skyscrapers are incompetent and criminally negligent. If what the government says about 9/11 is false, we have some work to do. Credit belongs to this group, and to the professions it represents, for taking up this difficult fight.

Independent research into 9/11 begins with skeptical, well reasoned assessments of official explanations. It does not end with that. Again, evolution of inquiry into Kennedy's assassination serves as a model for 9/11 researchers. What began as skepticism about the Warren Commission report evolved over years and decades into analysis of evidence that the official investigation ignored. Thirty years after the event, citizens demanded the government declassify records related to the murder. Fifty years after the event, numerous pieces of information assembled from multiple sources led to solid arguments that the Warren Commission was wrong.

Ultimately, government can and perhaps will have a role in uncovering what actually happened on 9/11. Under current conditions, however, no one in government would ever, ever permit an open, thorough, and truthful investigation of the events that occurred in New York City, Shanksville, and Washington, DC on that day. We are too close to the events, and government officials will not incriminate themselves. Neither would they do anything that compromises their ability to operate in secret.

Meantime, research conducted independently of government officials will continue – it must continue. Government would like the 9/11 truth movement to go away. We know that it will not, even if our republican freedoms continue to deteriorate. Part of the truth about 9/11, assembled in the United States and in other countries, has already convinced many citizens that the rest of the truth matters in this case. Part of the truth about 9/11 and other secret crimes is that people build an accurate picture of events collaboratively, over time, and that over time the picture improves and resolves. We know that, gradually, courageous people will compile evidence that places responsibility for 9/11 where it belongs.

Why Investigative Commissions Yield Fictional Accounts

The 9/11 attacks present numerous inexplicable problems – puzzles if you like – that invite us to engage in scientific reasoning. That means eliminating possibilities until you find the simplest one that fits the evidence. Process of elimination gives you accurate results if you know how to do it. That kind of reasoning explains what, at a first look, appears inexplicable. Why did U. S. air defenses fail? Why did the FAA not follow its standard procedures? Why did the debris at the Pentagon not include parts from a large passenger jet? Why was the debris near Shanksville spread over such a large area? Why did so many extended cell phone calls from the doomed planes come through, with such good reception? Who exactly were the people who executed the attacks? Why did three skyscrapers at the World Trade Center come down at free fall, or nearly free fall speeds? These puzzles don't answer themselves. These puzzles require fairly sophisticated reasoning if you attack them with tools designed to find the truth.

Interestingly, the commission President Bush appointed to investigate the 9/11 crimes did not address any of these questions in an orderly way. The commission treated the questions as irrelevant, already solved, ill defined or illegitimate. The commission actually had to presume the answer to one question: who planned and conducted the attacks? It resolved that one with no proof or any kind of demonstration at all, as the government had answered that one for us long before the commission commenced its work. You knew, before the president put his so-called investigators to work, how they would deal with the question of responsibility.

The 9/11 Commission's report

Given the simplicity of its charge – who did this to us? – you might expect a report from the commission that was pretty straightforward. People expected a couple of hundred pages. Any Washington hand can fill that much space with reasonable material, without embarrassment. Whatever the length, you want a report that states a question, or a set of related questions, and then applies recognized methods of logic and investigation to answer the questions.

Consider what the commission produced instead. Instead of honest, soundly researched answers about what actually happened, it's a government-issue, blame-free assessment of how the country can prevent such a thing from happening again. It contains virtually none of the information you would expect in a crime report. A sixth-grader could have given a better account of the day's events. The president might say, "So what? The commission did what I asked it to do, and that's what matters."

Not only did the investigation ignore apparently inexplicable elements of the case, it did not even take seriously the question of who carried out the attacks.

One reason for this failure is that government agencies did not want the commission to have evidence relevant to these questions. The investigators might have said, truthfully, "Of course the report is incomplete. Most of the relevant information is classified." In the end, though, that is not a satisfactory answer. Why, we might ask, is information related to this horrific crime classified? Why would government want to withhold information in this case?

The natural comparison in history for the 9/11 Commission is the Warren Commission in 1964. The difference between Lyndon Johnson and George W. Bush here is that Johnson launched the Warren Commission right away. Better to prove and approve the government's account sooner rather than later. Bush would have had no 9/11 Commission at all. He persistently opposed any investigation, by anyone, then authorized a commission only after Congress passed legislation for his signature. As the president did not explain why he resisted an investigation for so long, we can only guess. Vice-President Cheney pleaded that the effort would distract from the administration's Global War on Terror (GWOT).

That's an amazing excuse, when you look at it. It says, "We don't want to find out who attacked us, because that would distract us from the people we want to attack right now. That would be Iraq. If we attack the wrong people, that's our bad. Meantime, we want you to go away. Do not bother us anymore. Trust us, and be afraid. We have already told you what we want to tell you. You already know what you need to know." When the vice-president, who speaks for the president, gives you an excuse like that, you know it's a snow job. Public callousness does not become any high official after an attack like that. The White House's resistance to an investigation appeared odd, even by Dick Cheney's standards of transparency. Yet the amount of dishonesty that emanated from Bush's White House made the lack of an investigation appear almost routine.

The controlled demolition of World Trade Center 7 – passed off as an uncontrolled but simultaneous failure of the skyscraper's supporting columns – illustrates what I mean. No one could witness the destruction of this third skyscraper – on film or in person – and think it was anything other than planned. No forty-seven story skyscraper constructed of heavy steel could suddenly fall to the ground in just over seven seconds, due to normal fires in the lower half of the building. Just as government offered stock – and fictional – accounts to explain other puzzling elements of the 9/11 attacks, it offered essentially no explanation of World Trade Center 7's demolition. The building fell down at 5:20 pm, officials said: that's all you need to know.

When you see someone treat families of victims with that little respect, when you see families brushed off with financial settlements and confidentiality agreements to waive litigation, you are dealing with institutions that have no integrity. Victims' families say, "Honestly, won't you tell us more than that?" Government officials respond, implicitly, "We have already given you a lot of money. That should be enough for you." The first thing government officials do, after horrible events, is organize an ample victims' fund. It seems good hearted. Someday, we will see these dispensations as hush money, distributed on behalf of the national security state.

How should we respond to official crimes?

What should we think if we observe a prison camp that imprisons innocent people? That question arose when the United States government rounded up Japanese American citizens after Pearl Harbor, and put them in camps for the entire war. Are the guards in those camps innocent? What about the people who planned the camps, who employed the guards and gave orders to all the people required to run the camps? How would you bring those officials to account for what they did wrong?

We know that's a difficult problem to resolve, because the people who created those camps never were brought to account. No one responsible for maintaining, overseeing, funding, supplying, managing, staffing, or certifying the legality of those camps was ever asked, what the hell are you doing? How can you imprison American citizens without due process? Of course people did ask that question at the time, but no one in government had to – or bothered to – answer it.

What is the proper reaction of onlookers when trusted individuals or institutions in authority commit crimes? We have had some opportunity to consider that question in relation to Jerry Sandusky's activities at Penn State. Jerry Sandusky had an opportunity to carry out his crimes because he held a position of prestige in the university's revered football program. He had social immunity, as do church leaders and other leaders whom we respect because of their positions. We give some people benefit of the doubt.

An adult raping a young boy or girl is one of the worst crimes you can commit. Yet the more heinous the crime, the more our social brains and diffident hearts seem to find a way to overlook it. No one wants to make such a charge if one is not confident of support from others. Confronting criminals is awkward. We learned during Sandusky's trial that people at Penn State knew what he was doing for a long time. Yet they could not admit it, nor did they act on their uncomfortable perceptions and intuitions.

What if your own government starts to do things so patently criminal that you have to overlook these activities in order to function normally? Suppose we discover that people who hold respected positions in our government are actually criminals, that their crimes include assassination and serial murder, torture, ultra-secret operations, details of prisoner treatment that sicken you when you learn about them, and systematic violations of our Constitution? If you wanted to find out whether government officials had participated in crimes of that magnitude, how would you do that? Would you ask people in government to find out?

When something suspicious occurs out in the provinces, so to speak, government agencies typically investigate the possibility of foul play to determine what happened, how it happened, and who was involved. If government is the main suspect in a criminal case, you cannot ask government to investigate itself. The Warren Commission and the 9/11 Commission show you the results. Yet under our laws, government agencies are the only bodies with authority to conduct criminal investigations. Can government officials commit as many crimes as they like, because no independent authority exists to call the individuals who commit these crimes to account? The most disturbing thing to note is that these officials know they are not subject to the same laws they administer for everyone else. They know that, for the time being, what they do is hidden.

We have already observed that the people who lost their lives in the World Trade Center did not die because of structural weakness in the buildings they occupied. When two one-hundred-ten story towers built of steel and concrete blow up right in front of you, and a third forty-seven story building collapses into itself in a matter of seconds, you ask why something like that might occur. You ask why no one had to account for what happened in plain sight. One group of government experts says that fires in each building weakened the steel at critical points, causing a progressive collapse in all three buildings. Another group of experts, outside of government, says that jet fuel fires cannot melt steel. Even if they could, they point out, structural weakness high in a skyscraper would not cause steel supports to give way in the floors below.

Scientific reasoning

How can we turn the nature and purpose of scientific reasoning to good advantage here? Scientific enterprise – logic, experimentation and tests, evaluation of evidence – makes the inexplicable, explicable. Before science existed, magic, superstition, and naturally religion explained life's mysteries. Before science, the sun – the source of life on our planet – had no rational explanation. We did not know why it rose and set. We had no idea how it generated so much heat. Its ultimate source of energy is still a mystery.

Phenomena here on earth are more amenable to observation and analysis. The 9/11 attacks present numerous inexplicable problems – puzzles if you like – that invite us to engage in scientific reasoning. Only that kind of reasoning can explain what, at a first look, appears inexplicable. Two main puzzle, stated above, exist: 1) Who exactly were the people who executed the attacks? 2) Why did three steel framed skyscrapers at the World Trade Center come down at free fall, or nearly free fall speeds? These puzzles don't answer themselves. These puzzles require a certain kind of reasoning to solve. The reasoning required is fairly sophisticated, if you do it correctly.

Evidence and urgency

You may say, "Where's the evidence you refer to frequently? I see a lot of good analysis here, but detailed evidence appears pretty scant." I agree about that. I don't like duplication. *Infamy* does not include more evidence than it needs to make its points. It does not try to assemble extensive evidence from other sources. Rather, it introduces analyses, arguments and comparisons based on work other researchers have already done.

Back when libraries served as our main information repositories, some expectation existed that writers like me would bring obscure evidence out of those libraries, to make it accessible in a book. Now a great deal of material, including video evidence, is available with a few clicks. Anyone, anywhere has access now to resources once available only to researchers able to spend many hours in a large library. Initial finds will lead you to more resources than you thought existed. Learn what others know about the subjects discussed here. If you start with the best, theologians and philosophers like James Douglass and David Ray Griffin, the learning process does not take long.

Keep in mind a second point as well. It is allied with my desire not to recapitulate evidence available elsewhere. Several arguments take some questions as settled. For instance, we needn't revisit questions about the Warren Report's veracity. We have accumulated evidence – more than fifty years of curated evidence – to testify that the document does not contain an adequate account of how President Kennedy died. When you perceive that alternate accounts supersede the Warren Report, open and encouragingly fruitful exchanges about what actually did happen on November 22 can begin.

A parallel question exists regarding the events of September 11. We can, in fact, take the 9/11 Commission Report as incorrect and incomplete. That is an easy call. Page through the report, and you will find virtually no evidence: no evidence about 9/11, and no evidence that the commission conducted an investigation as such. *President Bush did not want the commission to conduct an investigation,* and it did not. The commission produced a general report about how to prevent an attack like 9/11 from happening again. To undertake a report like that when you do not know what actually happened – and moreover, when you do not care to know – is absurd. The commission draws conclusions about 9/11 before it takes any trouble to gather evidence. It clearly assumes that official accounts – publicized days after the attacks and fixed in place during subsequent months – are true.

Evidence about Kennedy's murder and the September 11 attacks differ in a key respect. We have had far less time to digest alternate accounts of the 2001 attacks. Our bodies – and minds – tell us we cannot rush digestion, but we can improve it. We can bite off small chunks. We can chew well. We can stay active and eat small amounts frequently rather than consume large feasts. We can stay calm and clear-eyed about our purposes, and reflect on what we know. We can rely on our friends for fellowship and help. If we follow these principles for ourselves and our research, our understanding of the 9/11 attacks will come along rapidly enough. We need to stay with the project, and digest steadily.

So even though September 11 happened less than a generation ago, not over two generations as in the case of Kennedy's assassination, we have come a long way in understanding both crimes. For 9/11, a lot of well known, respected professionals in many fields have voiced doubts about conventional accounts of the attacks. Abundant photographic evidence, coupled with interpretive, analytical, historical, scientific and eye-witness accounts all confirm that we have a lot of work to do.

If we let conventional accounts settle in due to an irresolute, what's-the-use lassitude, what do you think children born today will learn in their history classes fifteen years from now? It won't be the truth, because the state exercises a lot of guidance about what we teach them. That is why we need to be extra energetic and persistent, to develop alternate accounts closer to the truth.

We waited nearly two generations for the best accounts of Kennedy's murder to reach us. Even then, resistance to the truth remains. Some people even wonder why we should care about an assassination that happened such a long time ago. Those questions confirm why the struggle for truth about September 11 must remain urgent, focused, and active. The phrase *never forget* applies not only to victims of September 11 crimes, but also to revelation of truth about who committed them.

Rethink the Pancake Theory

Cues and associative memory affect our perceptions. They function as interpretive frameworks for visual evidence. Psychologists have done various, sometimes mundane and sometimes ingenious experiments to test for this relationship. It turns out that remembered cues do affect the way we interpret evidence. The connection is so strong, in fact, that it can cause us to reach incorrect conclusions. Perceptually valid, accurately recalled cues can cause us to misinterpret evidence. That's why it pays to compare interpretations among people who bring different cues to the same set of observations.

Frameworks of perception

When frameworks help us connect familiar with unfamiliar observations, they work efficiently to help us make sense of new phenomena. The difficulty is, we don't have a framework for what we saw when the Twin Towers came down. Airliners don't crash into one hundred story buildings. We certainly had not seen 110-story skyscrapers explode progressively from the top down before that day. If someone speaks with authority about what we have seen, we have scant grounds to doubt the explanation if we cannot compare the authority's evidence with something we have seen before.

After the attacks, the authoritative explanation for the towers' destruction does not take long to come. Heat from jet fuel fires weakens the steel columns and trusses that form the skeleton of each tower. When these structural columns and their associated joints give way, the entire tower collapses in a pancake effect: each story fails after the one above it fails, due to the unnatural amount of weight coming down on top of it. Thus both towers fall straight down.

The explanation sounds plausible enough. Evidence for this kind of collapse in a steel framed building does not exist, for it has never happened before. Moreover, no competing theories came forth in the days that followed the catastrophe. The wreckage did not yield evidence relevant to this novel theory, so before long we had computer models to show how the pancake effect would have worked. Computer models carry a lot of authority, partly because the people who develop them seem smarter than we are, partly because computers seem such mysteriously intelligent machines. Those impressions serve computer modelers well.

The pancake theory has a few difficulties that make it implausible. First, the buildings' progressive destruction does not begin at the crash sites. For both towers, the destruction begins at the top of the building. Second, the weight from the upper stories does not bear directly down. The upper stories explode multi-directionally into dust and pieces of steel. The concrete disappears into fine dust, and the structural steel flies outward. The explosions start at the top of the buildings, above the crash sites, and continue past the crash sites as they advance toward the ground. Clearly, the structural steel below the explosions does not bear more weight than it did while the buildings were whole. The explosions remove weight from the top of the structure.

Admittedly, to describe the destruction at the top and all the way down the towers as explosions begs the question. They look like explosions, but perhaps pancaking, which we've never seen before, looks like a progressive explosion. Pancaking would not turn all of that concrete to dust, but we can leave that point for now. Let's take a look at another difficulty: the rate of destruction.

The rate of collapse does not beg any questions about what we are seeing. Each tower comes down in a little over twelve seconds. Using a round figure of one hundred stories for the building height, each story pancaked in about 0.12 seconds, or about one-eighth of a second per story. For comparison, Usain Bolt's Olympic time in the 100 meter sprint is 9.63 seconds. Mr. Bolt takes just over four steps per second when he runs, which means each step requires about 0.24 seconds. The pancake theory requires us to accept that, by weight alone, the structural steel in each story of these gargantuan buildings collapsed in half the time

Mr. Bolt requires for one step, when he sprints at a world record pace.

Here are some more rough calculations. Each tower lost about eight stories per second. Each story in the towers was a little under four meters tall. That tells us the towers came down at about thirty-two meters per second, or three times Bolt's velocity when he sprints at top speed. We know how fast he runs.

Suppose each floor takes only one half second to collapse. Then the building requires fifty-five seconds, not twelve, to come down. Twelve seconds to destroy a one-hundred-ten-story, steel-framed building is awfully fast. A two-story wooden house that has burned to the point of structural weakness takes longer than twelve seconds to collapse. We know that each tower contained 78,000 tons of structural steel. Below the crash sites, each tower was structurally sound. If the architects designed a building that could collapse that fast – whatever trauma it might have suffered – they designed a catastrophically unsafe building. The idea that towers that size could collapse in twelve seconds by gravity alone is not plausible. The theory implies that, as the building fell, its steel frame offered no more resistance than air.

The interpretive framework in the government's explanation for why the towers came down is incorrect. It refers to a pancake effect that is plainly wrong. A bit more technically, the official explanation claims that the horizontal trusses that support each column unzipped from the building's vertical columns due to the unusual stresses placed on the building's structural components. This explanation is equally implausible. We should recognize our mistake in accepting outlandish interpretive frameworks, understand why we erred, then work toward more plausible explanations.

An alternate hypothesis proposes that the buildings exploded, from the top down. This explanation suggests that explosions removed the core columns at the base of the towers as well. Can controlled explosions explain how the Twin Towers fell in twelve seconds – about eight floors per second – better than the pancake hypothesis? Architects and structural engineers who have studied this problem closely believe the government's explanations for structural failure are inferior. More than that, they are deceptive. In light of evidence and explanations available from all sources, can we reinterpret existing cues, and fashion new frameworks for what we saw on 9/11? Can we rethink what we see in the video evidence, in order to re-perceive the process of destruction?

Vertical strength in steel-framed skyscrapers

Government officials forfeit trust when they conceal or destroy evidence of political crimes. The great thing about photographs and video recordings – especially in the age of the internet – is that these are not so easily destroyed. Government has proven that it can keep certain categories of evidence off the internet. Nevertheless, people involved in crimes have a harder time than they did before, when they try to disguise involvement.

Someday we will say, "How did we think this destruction was anything other than a controlled series of explosions?" Put another way, how could we think that gravity – by itself – brought down all 110 stories of this skyscraper? We make ourselves believe one thing, because the alternative is too awful.

Sometimes simple analysis yields clear results. Consider the pancake-zipper theory, used to explain how each tower fell straight down long after jet fuel fires ignited the upper floors. The theory has a certain plausibility, if you concentrate on certain parts of the evidence. The first key element of the theory is that the collapse of the upper floors initiates a chain reaction, whereby the collapse of each floor causes the floor below it to fail. The second key concept proposes that the horizontal trusses supporting each floor detach sequentially, or unzip from the vertical columns as the weight of the pancaking floors above come down on them. Not designed for that amount of vertical strain, the trusses detach from the inner and outer columns floor by floor, until the zipper effect reaches ground level.

Now consider the building in its standing state, where we can analyze structural integrity and vertical strength in a static setting. To pick round numbers, the columns and trusses in the first ten stories bear the weight of one hundred stories above them. The columns and horizontal supports in the lower floors bear the weight of all the floors above. That is why the column thickness at the base so exceeds column thickness near the top. The base bears so much more weight. It bears that weight securely, no matter how much the top of the building might sway due to high winds. It bears that weight securely, even if an airplane crashes into an upper floor. A disturbance, trauma, or other unusual condition at the ninety-first floor does not affect the integrity of the base. It does not affect the base's ability to support the weight it always supported.

Now we come to a key point about this kind of structure. The force of gravity cannot "unzip" a rectangular, steel-framed skyscraper, no matter what damage occurs to the upper floors. To pretend that the lower half of a steel-framed skyscraper can destroy itself after the building suffers damage to its upper floors, is both fantasy and improvisation. No one who understands the architecture of the North and South towers can find the pancake-zipper theory believable. Steel-framed buildings are too strong to come down spontaneously or unintentionally, no matter how much damage occurs in the upper floors.

A rectangular, steel-framed tower is built to maintain its integrity in the lower floors. Catastrophic damage to upper floors does not affect that integrity. To grasp this point, compare an arch with a Lego tower. An arch has a keystone at the top, the last stone the builder places. Remove the keystone, or any other stone in the arch for that matter, and the structure fails. The integrity that gives the arch strength to hold so much weight disappears. Unlike an arch, a rectangular structure does not permit empty space underneath, but neither does it depend on every component remaining in place to retain its vertical strength. Build a rectangular tower of Lego bricks, then press down on it from the top. It will never give way. Remove some bricks three-quarters of the way up. You may have weakened the tower at that point, but you have not damaged the integrity or strength of the tower below that point.

The internal reinforcements in a steel-framed tower give the structure the same robust resistance to vertical pressure. That is why we consider skyscrapers constructed of steel, glass and concrete such a miracle of architecture, an eye-catching demonstration of our ability to conquer vertical space, and gravity, with materials so substantial we can live in the air a thousand feet above ground. You cannot make a tower constructed with steel columns collapse from the top down, by gravity or by any other natural force. To destroy a tower like that, you have to destroy the integrity of its internal reinforcements. You have to break the columns, not in one place, but throughout the structure.

One more observation: the pancake-zipper theory holds that by the time the destructive chain reaction reaches, say, the fortieth floor, the extraordinary strain on the trusses from dozens of floors pancaking down, one after another, causes all of the truss joints on the given floor to fail simultaneously. The same happens at floor thirty-nine, then thirty-eight, until you reach the ground. When you look at video recordings of the Twin Towers coming down, however, you don't see extra weight from falling floors causing a progressive collapse from the top of the building to the bottom. In fact, you don't see any weight at all. By the time the destruction reaches the bottom half of the building, what used to be the building above is just a toadstool-shaped ball of dust and debris. The weight the lower floors bear when the pancake-zipper theory says they must collapse, is far less than the weight they bear when the building stands in its normal state. In fact, the weight they bear near the end of the progressive destruction is almost nothing.

What then accounts for this progressive destruction, first of the building's upper floors, and then its base? Before you answer that question, ask why cleanup workers found so much molten steel underneath the ruins at ground zero. Ask where that amount of subterranean thermal energy could have originated. It was not left-over jet fuel, which had largely burned off by the time the towers came down. It was not solar energy, or geo-thermal energy. Heat sufficient to melt steel to liquid helped destroy the buildings' structural integrity. For each skyscraper, that energy originated in and contributed to a destructive process that began well after the buildings suffered damage to their upper floors. When the destructive process commences, you see something new in the events of that morning. The jet fuel fires do not initiate or cause the process of destruction that follows.

Double Standards, Deceptive Logic, and Ridicule

What is intellectual dishonesty? It is not exactly the same as lying. Here are three forms of it:

Double ethical standard. In public discussion, the double standard often shows itself as a claim that I can do what I like, because I am in the right to begin with. Other people have to follow rules that don't apply to me.

Deceptive logic. Poor reasoning covers numerous errors. A general form of this error reasons from conclusions to evidence. That is, you assess evidence only in light of where you want to be at the end of your argument.

Ridicule. This form often begins with epithets or language chosen to place your opponents at a disadvantage. It often ends with dismissiveness and contempt.

Double ethical standard

One type of dishonesty reveals itself as a particularly pernicious double standard: I don't have to follow the same rules you have to follow, because I am right, and the things I want to do are necessary to defend the truth. By contrast, you are wrong, and you must not be permitted to spread falsehood. That is the essential position of Cass Sunstein, a University of Chicago law professor and friend of President Obama. Sunstein advocates infiltration of groups that seek a new investigation of 9/11, in order to disrupt those groups, sow division, spread false rumors and accusations, and generally render ineffective the activities of people who cannot build bonds of face-to-face trust.

These are exactly the tactics that Communist and other totalitarian parties used to maintain their power for so long. Sunstein's only justification for these clearly unconstitutional actions is that the groups he opposes as harmful must be suppressed. They must be suppressed because what they advocate endangers the state. It is the same self-righteousness that tyrants consistently use to cloak their power with fake legitimacy: we can do anything we like, because we have right on our side. We have to do these things to protect whatever public good we happen to advocate at the moment.

Cass Sunstein's *Conspiracy Theories* illustrates this way of thinking. For a thorough deconstruction of Sunstein's thinking, see David Ray Griffin's *Cognitive Infiltration: An Obama Appointee's Plan to Undermine the 9/11 Conspiracy Theory*. Sunstein's essay looks impressive when you pick it up. It's fitted out with an abstract, footnotes, and a bibliography. It's also laced with authorial arrogance, as if he wants to add, "I don't really want to spend that much time with this question, but in the end it's important, so I'll do it."

The article discusses how we should respond to conspiracy theories. Because false conspiracy theories have pernicious effects, Sunstein says we can't let them stand unchallenged. For instance, government should undermine accounts of 9/11 that suggest it was a false flag operation. We can't let people believe in false theories that make them wonder whether the government is guilty of such criminal acts, Sunstein suggests. Sunstein wrote the paper not long before President Obama hired Sunstein to help him make the government look good.

The interesting thing about this paper, published in the *Journal of Political Philosophy* in 2009, is that Sunstein has nothing to say about how we tell whether or not a conspiracy theory is false. He acknowledges that some conspiracy theories are true, but suggests that most are false. He does not explain why government's account of 9/11 – which maintains that enemies in Afghanistan conspired to attack New York City – qualifies as a true conspiracy theory. He believes other accounts of 9/11 – accounts that challenge the government's conspiracy theory – to be false. Indeed, he compares other accounts to parents' conspiracy theory about Santa Claus.

This latter comparison merely substitutes ridicule for argumentation. If you can paint your opponents as foolish, perhaps you do not need to engage them. Sunstein needs to explain why he thinks most conspiracy theories are false, and some are true. Without solid reasoning in that vein, Sunstein's self assurance does him in.

One comparison we might consider is that between cognitive infiltration and old-fashioned, physical infiltration. Cognitive infiltration, in plain language, means to get inside someone's head! You want to confuse people so they no longer feel sure about what is true and what is false. Then you can lead them to trust or at least accept government again, rather than fellow conspiracy theorists. Sowing confusion requires techniques that western democracies have generally not used against their own citizens.

Here Sunstein illustrates clearly how ungrounded self assurance results in a double standard. If you're confident 9/11 conspiracy theories are false, and that they threaten the state's foundations, you begin to think of ways to counteract their influence, even if your proposals are illegal. Sunstein's concern about reputational harm from 9/11 conspiracy theories, makes him promote illegal conduct that would damage government's reputation even more.

Deceptive logic

A second type of intellectual dishonesty is deceptive logic, and methods of inquiry that support such logic. Here Philip Zelikow, executive director of the 9/11 commission, serves as a good example. Zelikow was charged by Congress and the president to find out what happened on 9/11. He wanted to give clear direction to his investigators before they began their work. Any researcher would say that to plan your work, you would write a list of questions you want to investigate. To maintain a sense of structure, you might organize your questions into those you want to tackle first, and those you want to tackle later. You would not presuppose answers to any of your questions. You would, rather, think about what resources you need to locate in order to answer your questions. You might do the same kind of planning for your hypotheses: which ones will you tackle first, and what do you need to test them?

How did Zelikow accomplish these planning tasks? He wrote a detailed outline of the commission's report before his investigators began their research. The outline did not contain any questions or hypotheses. It contained answers to questions. He had heard people ask, how could this happen, and how can we prevent it from happening again? Zelikow outlined a report that would give general, non-controversial responses to these questions. The people who prepared the report knew its contents before they gathered any information. That is not an investigation. The polite term for a report like that is a snow job, based on transparently dishonest logic. Less politely, one might call such an investigation a fraud, clothed in the prestige of government.

Ridicule

The last type of dishonesty is ridicule. People who use ridicule are hypocrites. They pretend to be better than you are, when they are not better. They use names as weapons, calling you a truther, or a denier, or behind your back, a conspiracy nut. A conspiracy nut does not deserve any attention at all, certainly not from superiors. Hypocrites consider themselves superior, for people who hold certain beliefs must be stupid. You see now why hypocrites and conspiracy nuts do not communicate with each other. Communication requires reciprocal respect. Hypocrites talk only to each other.

Recognize these forms of dishonesty when you see them. With that recognition, you gain emotional resources to speak articulately when you encounter forceful people who practice these types of dishonesty. At a minimum, you can understand how their minds operate, and use that understanding to evaluate their arguments.

Crass Conspiracy Theories

How is anti-Semitic sentiment connected to 9/11? Preliminary to this question, note that in every area of American culture, anti-Semitism is submerged. Seventy-five to a hundred years ago, if you were white, male, heterosexual, and Protestant, you were set: a made man. If you were Jewish, or black, or Catholic, or Irish, or Italian, or gay, or female, you developed – consciously or otherwise – a means of interacting with the dominant, in group. When we come to a political crime like 9/11, a crime that occurs long after these socially calcified structures and prejudices have begun to break down, we see how the scum of anti-Semitism floats to the surface in little colonies. Social trauma and fear seem to grant people leeway to voice animosities they would otherwise keep closeted. After the 9/11 attacks, we saw a rise in anti-Arab sentiment, loose fear easily converted to hate, and hate easily converted to fear.

When you look further into who committed these crimes, you needn't look far before you encounter the word *Zionist*. That is the preferred term, substituted for Jew, Israeli, or any other label one might want to apply to suspected villains. One could be mistaken about this use of the word, but why would you choose that word when you make accusations about who was responsible for 9/11? If you want to identify a group in the twenty-first century, why choose a label that refers to a nineteenth-century movement to establish a Jewish homeland in the Middle East? You may as well call a Catholic a *papist*, when the subject of discussion has nothing to do with Rome, the Vatican, or the pope.

Without exception, people who raise the Zionist specter when they write about 9/11 do so with one thing in mind: to place blame. They believe the crime grows out of a Jewish conspiracy. In that way, the parallel with the Reichstag fire of 1933, in Berlin, is telling. Germans wanted to blame the fire on the Jews and the Communists, their favorite bogeymen and international conspirators, even though they had no evidence for the charge. Similarly, some people here in the United States seem ready to blame a Zionist conspiracy for the events of 9/11, even though you can look carefully and find no solid evidence to support the accusation.

Let's take one piece of evidence these generally nameless accusers bring forward to validate their idea that an international Zionist conspiracy lay behind the 9/11 attacks. The evidence cited is that Jewish office workers at the World Trade Center received messages – warnings – early on September 11 or the day before not to go to work. No one has produced a sample of one of these messages. No one has named one sender or recipient of such a message. Yet the rumor about the warning messages is out there. It doesn't go away. When you run across it, you see that it tends to accompany other ugly innuendo.

Innuendo and rumors do not constitute satisfactory evidence. They are not evidence at all. Yet one wants to ask, what is the origin of a rumor like that? Who put it out there, and why? What purpose does it serve?

As a test of the anti-Zionist argument, let's grant for the moment that the rumor is true. Jewish workers at the World Trade Center did receive messages early on September 11, warning them not to go to work that day. What would that signify? Would it signify that an international Jewish conspiracy planned to blow up the World Trade Center that day, in order to advance some unknown purpose? Under the principle of "anything's possible," I suppose you can't rule that one out, though one could also say that given the provenance of this theory, we should not waste time with it.

The rumor about the warning messages, if true, has a more likely interpretation. Let's say that World Trade Center workers actually did receive these messages, and that these warnings indicate insiders knew about 9/11 in advance. Who are insiders in this case? Intelligence agencies have access to inside information. That's their business. What intelligence agencies have a close working relationship? The CIA and Israel's Mossad share information all the time. If the CIA knew about the 9/11 attacks in advance, chances are good that people in Israel's intelligence establishment knew about them as well. Intelligence agencies manage secret information, but they employ human beings, so they often leak. If the Mossad knew about the 9/11 attacks in advance, wouldn't you expect that a single leak of that information would blossom into a series of warning messages to office workers?

Does that digital phone tree of messages give evidence of an international Zionist conspiracy behind the 9/11 attacks? Of course not. It means that inside information from the United States government made its way to some people's cell phone shortly before the attacks. Normally that kind of leak is unremarkable, as they happen so frequently. In this case the leak, if it happened, indicates advance knowledge of a world-historic attack. That is significant. The lead does not, however, indicate that the attack resulted from a Zionist conspiracy. When you add that kind of trash to the mix, you're likely to dismiss the rumor without even checking it out.

For 9/11, evidence of advance knowledge appears everywhere you look:

- President Bush continues to read in the Florida classroom after the first attack: the Secret Service is supposed to protect the president immediately when an attack occurs.
- Air defense training exercise planned the morning of the attacks.
- Suspension of all air defense standard procedures after the attacks were underway.
- Numerous warnings ahead of time that higher-ups chose to ignore.
- Higher-ups who failed to prevent the attacks rewarded and promoted rather than fired.
- Osama bin Laden fingered immediately after the attacks, with no investigation to determine what actually happened.
- Knowledge of the destruction of World Trade Center 7 is all over the place on the afternoon of September 11, well before it falls at 5:20 pm.

- Advocacy for a new Pearl Harbor by key higher-ups in the Project for the New American Century.
- Government carefully controls all information related to the crime, after it happens.

The warning messages to World Trade Center workers fit this larger pattern. Yet because the messages became grist for anti-Zionist conspiracy theories, independent researchers do not care to check them out. You would have to find only one message to substantiate the rumor. The message would show the sender, the recipient, and the date. If the NSA doesn't have that metadata, then who does? Submit a Freedom of Information Act request to the NSA for those messages, and see how they respond.

This kidding reference to the NSA does highlight a difficulty with finding even one warning message. No sender or recipient wants to stand up and give names at this point: why take a chance like that? The feds have charged people under the Espionage Act for less. So if those warning messages do exist, they'll likely remain hidden, the subject of rumor. Most of all, we should not think of them as evidence of a conspiracy. If they exist, they are evidence of advance knowledge of the attacks. That is valuable evidence to have.

To conclude, then, we have in the anti-Zionist charges a category error. Suppose you suspect the Mossad, Israel's secret intelligence service, of being involved in 9/11. Suppose you have hints that the Mossad, along with parts of the United States government, collaborated in the crime. I would say, so what? We know Mossad agents commit crimes. They assassinate people, and engage in other secret activities. We have quite a bit of evidence that members of the Mossad undertake dirty work for the Israeli state. The problem is, they undertake these activities because they are members of a secret intelligence service, not because they are Jews. They serve the Israeli state, and in that role they act like other secret agents who serve their states. They do not commit crimes to serve an international Jewish conspiracy.

The anti-Zionists can readily say, "Yes, but the Israeli state is by definition Zionist, so it's okay to use that label as we make our accusations." Not so: if you have a problem with the Mossad, make your charges against that organization, and show the evidence. If you have a problem with the Israeli state, make your charges against Israel and its leaders. Show the evidence. When you make your charges against Zionists, you might as well accuse all Jews, given the label you have selected. The Protocols of the Elders of Zion, the infamously anti-Semitic, fraudulent tract, serves as the source of the label in modern political discourse. When you use the word Zionist, you borrow from a long tradition of anti-Jewish propaganda, hatred, and agitation.

I hardly have to add that the scummy growth of anti-Zionist accusations on the surface of political discussions concerning 9/11 does no favor for people skeptical of the government's account. Defenders of the official account look for any means to cast doubt on skeptics' reasonableness. Defenders of the official account simply group skeptics with anti-Zionists, to discredit the whole lot. Moreover, anyone who wants to find the truth about 9/11 quickly runs into the anti-Zionist conspiracy theories. The individual asks, "What am I getting into here?" In that environment, the value of good evidence and sound reasoning increases.

We have to decide what to ignore, and where to concentrate effort. Close analysis of the 9/11 Commission's report does not seem a good use of time. For surprisingly similar reasons, anti-Zionist conspiracy theories also waste our time. Both accounts ignore evidence, practice poor logic, and play to deep loyalties. These loyalties respond well to propaganda. As we evaluate various accounts and arguments, we ought to use our appreciation, even instinct for rationality to identify narratives that point toward the truth, and applaud analysts who care about the truth.

Anti-Zionist theories fall into the opposite category. They build on long established histories of suspicion and prejudice to make their case. They have no evidence of substance to underpin their accusations. Moreover, they cannot tell a story that makes any sense, or that is persuasive to anyone who looks for dispassionate reasoning in a complicated case like this one.

To Hell With What People Think: This Is War

On September 18, 1931, the Japanese detonated some dynamite near their railway in Mukden, Manchuria. They blamed the sabotage on the Chinese, using the pretend attack as a pretext to occupy the entire province. The staged event became known as the Mukden Incident. It's a good example of a false flag attack. Reduced to its simplest terms, the phrase means: blow something up and blame it on your enemy. You plant your opponent's flag on your own crime.

Interestingly, the people who perpetrate false flag attacks generally care little whether their criminal demonstrations convince or fool people. The Japanese didn't care that other countries in the region and overseas immediately suspected them of a malign, self-serving swindle. Briskly, the Japanese marched out of the League of Nations and into Manchuria. Actually, they did it the other way around: they erected their puppet state, named Manchukuo, in 1932, then left the League in 1933. When you aim to build an empire, or just stir up trouble, you don't actually need to bother with the international community. Bring it on.

If you don't care about perceptions, you might ask, why bother with a false flag attack to begin with? A false flag attack does build fear and warm feelings for revenge at home. More than that, it gins up hatred, war fever, a willingness to march away and slay new enemies by the scores. Japan's war planners needed backing in Tokyo, Osaka, and Kyoto, not sympathy from the international community. If you can make your own families and your own cities feel they are under attack, that's what counts. For these purposes, Mukden succeeded. Six and half years after the fireworks in Mukden, the Japanese marched into Nanjing and raped it. Two and a half years after that, Japanese torpedo bombers attacked Pearl Harbor. Eventually, Japan's own cities came under attack.

Planners used more than a few sticks of explosives to destroy the Twin Towers and World Trade Center 7. Beyond the difference in scale, we see a couple of key similarities in the attacks. First, other countries soon came to see each attack for what it was. The so-called victim was complicit. Second, leaders used the attacks to build support for war. Japan wanted war against China. The U. S. wanted war against Iraq. The so-called victim, lowly and betrodden like a serpent, launched its attack swiftly enough.

Astonishingly, planners in the U. S. seemed not to care about the impact of their actions overseas. They truly did not care what others overseas thought. Unlike Japan, which strove to build an empire in its part of the world, the United States already dominated the entire globe: culturally, militarily, economically, and of course politically. No nation had ever exercised so much influence and power for so long a period. No great power had ever equaled its reach. No great power had ever had so much to lose through stupidity, hubris, and recklessness. Yet the United States threw its empire and leadership away so it could go to war against two poor, weak states in the Middle East and south Asia: Iraq and Afghanistan. It created the conditions for aggressive military action, and did not care what anyone thought about either the conquest or the pretext for it.

We can see how much the people who blew up those buildings care what other people think when we consider their response to questions about the attacks:

Why don't we see evidence that a large airliner crashed into the side of the Pentagon?

Ignore reports about what you can see and what you can't see. Believe us, it happened. An airliner flew into the Pentagon.

Why don't we have more information about the nineteen hijackers?

We put out a list of all the hijackers right away.

Why did some of the people on the list turn up alive and well in the Middle East?

We don't know about that, but as soon as we found out, we put out a new list.

Why do we see the Twin Towers blow up right in front of us?

We say steel-framed skyscrapers pancaked down, one floor at a time, in a chain reaction. You claim you heard explosions in those buildings, and you wonder how the steel melted to liquid. You need not ask these skeptical questions – our experts have already dealt with them. Read their report.

Why don't we see evidence that an airliner crashed in a field near Shanksville, Pennsylvania? Why is the debris scattered over miles, as if the plane blew up in the air?

Why would you detract from the heroism of the patriots who took control of that plane and sacrificed their lives for you and all of us?

Why did the president read to those school children for so long, when everyone knew the country was under attack? Why would he act as if nothing unusual had happened, with his Secret Service detail standing by instead of protecting him?

We're not sure about that one.

Why did World Trade Center 7 come down in free fall when nothing hit it?

If you ask us to explain how the destruction of this building was anything but a controlled demolition, we have nothing to say beyond our report. Besides, what difference would it make if WTC 7 *did* come down intentionally? Sometimes buildings need to be destroyed.

Other questions come to mind, of course, as well as other unhelpful or impolite responses. Yet we cannot overlook the depressing but true point: someone blew up those buildings, and did not care that much how it came across. When you succeed with such an attack, you put your energy into the subsequent conquest, not the pretext. That's what George Bush meant when he said we should not investigate the 9/11 attacks, as that would distract us from the war on terror. The pretext – something abrupt and scary to rally people – enters the record only as a starting gun. It sends us forth with an ill but brisk wind at our backs.

Whatever the war planners think, the reaction of people in the rest of the world matters. What citizens here in the United States think matters. If our government's story about why the Twin Towers fell is false, and our government suppresses the truth, it won't survive. If our government's account is false, and it acts soon to discover or uncover the truth, it can still save itself. Do you see any evidence, past or present, that it is interested in the truth?

A great deal of 9/11 research to this point has concentrated on the question, what happened? Credible research by people with integrity, like David Ray Griffin, demonstrates that the government's account of what happened is false. The government's response to that research, in so few words, is "So what?" That is just how President Bush responded when people asked him why we should go to war against Iraq, if it did not have weapons that pose a danger to us. He said "So what?" Another version of this response is "What difference does it make?" With this response, war planners aim to shut you up. The subtext for people like Cheney and other vulcans is, "I'm engaged in something important here. Get out of my way, you little pipsqueak."

As you can see, Infamy does not revisit all the evidence that shows the government's account of 9/11 is false. Griffin's work validates this counter-claim: that whatever happened on 9/11, it does not conform to the official story. To use standard scientific terminology, Griffin falsifies the 9/11 Commission's hypothesis. That work is done.

I do want to answer the government's *so what* question. We can't let dismissive war planners hold the floor indefinitely after they issue their challenge. Someone has to engage them in this point. Someone has to answer the so what question, and follow that argument with another challenge: what now? What do we do, now that we have discovered what the war planners have done? We did not answer that question after the coup in 1963, nor did we respond to it after the Mukden incident at the World Trade Center. It's time.

Magical, Murderous Guardians

A lot of observers said that hurricane Sandy reminds us how much we rely on governments to protect us. They even used the storm to say critics of the nanny state are wrong-headed. You almost don't know where to start with arguments like that. The government doesn't protect us: we protect us. We establish various public institutions to carry out numerous cooperative activities, just as we form private institutions to carry out other cooperative activities. We don't say that business corporations protect us, as if they have some sort of life apart from us. Neither should we ever regard government as some kind of abstract, protective entity that exists apart from us.

Yet we seem to have an in-built instinct to regard government as a replacement parent. When we leave home, who will take care of us? How does it feel, to be a rolling stone? When we're on our own, don't we need someone to watch over us, to help us out when trouble comes? Life brings loneliness and estrangement, and we don't want to be alone. We want to belong to something, for security and protection.

If you agree with the premises of self-government, you know this way of thinking is dangerous in the extreme. Loneliness is real and natural, but finding comfort in the state is not. The potent state is not your friend. It runs a kind of legalized protection racket. Of all the threats you will face in your life – from nature, from criminals, from financial uncertainty, from people who act like your friend but turn out to be otherwise – an over-powerful, out of control state is the biggest threat of all.

The racket succeeds partly because the state appears to be something it is not. It pretends to exist to protect you, but that is not its purpose. As long as you keep quiet, it is primarily interested in your money. That's how an extortion racket works. The wolf – interested in food, not money – dressed himself up to look like granny – read nanny – to deceive Red Riding Hood. If successful, he devours a tender meal, even better than the first. The state behaves the same way. Its agents pretend to be your friend. In this kind of relationship, submission to the state's writ brings endless trouble, for the state will never let you alone. Any stance other than submission brings even more trouble, for people who resist the state's power must be broken.

Consider other stories to see how deeply we crave and appreciate protection, both as children and as adults. Hansel and Gretel is a particularly scary tale, as a heartless stepmother forces a poor woodcutter to take his children out into the woods to abandon them there. They wanted to trust their father, but he abandoned them in the woods. Only the children's ingenuity, courage, and perseverance save them: no one else will do it. Children love this story, frightening as it is, because brother and sister defeat the wicked witch on their own. They stick together and find a way out.

Cinderella's treatment was equally miserable, but she stayed hopeful. As Cinderella's stepmother and stepsisters exploited her, abused her and ostracized her, she kept a cheerful outlook and hoped for better times to come. Her fairy godmother, equipped with all kinds of supernatural powers, arranged for her to meet the prince, so one day she would be queen. Cinderella had someone looking after her, and her magical guardian came through.

One of the most compelling stories for young people in American literature, *To Kill a Mockingbird*, relies on this theme. "Hey Boo," says Scout as she recognizes Boo Radley standing in the corner. He has just rescued Scout and her brother Jem from Bob Ewell, who aimed to kill them as they walked home from a Halloween party. "Heck, someone's been after my children," says Atticus when he calls the sheriff. Shortly afterward, Atticus thanks Boo: "Thank you for my children." Mr. Radley – the amazing guardian angel, the mysterious neighbor who somehow knew the children needed his help – responds in silence.

Dumbledore and Harry's parents through all seven Harry Potter books, Odysseus when he returns home to Penelope in the Odyssey, Moses' leading his people out of Egypt to the Promised Land in Exodus: we find this theme of protection and bravery everywhere. Our favorite stories show the theme's power to compel our hearts and our attention.

Let's return to government and the kind of protection it offers. It gives you a helmet before it sends you into war. When the state wants to start a war, it wants your sons as well as your money. I recently completed Barbara Tuchman's *A Distant Mirror*, a book that – like her others – contains a lot of wisdom. By her account, the French serfs in the fourteenth century wanted so much to see their king as their protector. They knew the king and his nobles exploited them. Taxes, warfare, robbery, all kinds of injustice flowed from society's top ranks down upon the poor. The underclass resisted and revolted, several times. Even so, they hoped the king would come through to protect them. The king even dramatized his protective role at public festivals. Despite all contrary evidence, the people perceived the king, ordained by God, as the sovereign power who could redeem them from apparently inescapable misery.

Now let me tell you another story. Like Barbara Tuchman's, this one is real – not a fantasy, a myth, or a fairy tale. Here's a story filled with so much horror for grown-ups, they cannot stand to face it. Some months ago I watched a film titled *Explosive Evidence*, which investigates why two steel framed skyscrapers in the World Trade Center exploded on September 11, 2001, and why a third skyscraper imploded. A segment toward the film's end explores why people resist the conclusion that gravity did not bring these buildings down. "It can't be true," they say. One woman, when she realized how the buildings fell, took a long walk outside her office building. She said she could not stop sobbing as she walked block after block.

She became so upset because, until then, she had thought of government as her protector. The idea that it could be anything else wrenched her world view, forced her to see that it did not necessarily act as a replacement parent. She felt as Hansel and Gretel felt when they overheard their stepmother persuade their father to take them into the wilderness to let them starve. But for that bit of eavesdropping, Hansel would not have brought bread crumbs with him. From beginning to end, Hansel and Gretel managed to save themselves because they learned the truth, about their own home and about the witch's home. Like the woman in *Explosive Evidence* and the resourceful heroes of our favorite stories, we must recognize the truth about who means us harm, and use our wits to save ourselves.

Part Three:

Analysis of Political Crimes

Moments of Truth

Why did Bill Cosby's sexual predation take so long to come to light? One observer remarked, "People didn't want to live in a world where Cliff Huxtable was a rapist." More disturbing, does anyone want to live in a world where America's favorite dad is a rapist, yet no one acknowledges it? Now imagine a political crime committed against a whole nation, as destructive as rape committed by a powerful man against a woman. What is worse and what is better: to acknowledge what actually happened, or pretend nothing's wrong when courageous people say, something *is* wrong?

As Hannibal Burress said on stage, "You'll never be able to watch the *Cosby Show* the same way again."

It's like a social truth serum in reverse. These implicit, anesthetic social agreements hold for famous actors who drug and rape women, for political actors who demolish buildings to hide larger crimes, and for a killer who knocks off a patsy in a police station to preserve a false story about who murdered a president. These actors are so powerful that many people want to pretend the king has all of his clothes on, when he is obviously parading himself around town with nothing on at all. To point out that the president is naked is to invite public ridicule, even censure. People who say what is obviously true become truthers, extremists, fringe characters: people you don't want to associate with. Why not? Because if you do associate with them, no one will want to associate with you.

Common perception holds that high profile political crimes necessarily mean moments of supreme dishonesty. The crimes seem to foster comprehensive cover-ups, investigative commissions that merely pretend to find the truth, every kind of secrecy, misdirection and obfuscation, and often identification of a villain who becomes the nation's scapegoat. These dishonest, fraudulent campaigns do in fact follow political crimes, but we ought to perceive the crimes themselves as moments of high truth. Organizations and people that normally operate in secret, reveal themselves through acts that betray a kind of hubris and recklessness not often seen.

What except hubris, and a reckless disregard for appearances, can explain bringing down a forty-seven story skyscraper, World Trade Center 7, in seven seconds, and claiming the cause was anything but a controlled demolition? What except hubris, and a reckless disregard for appearances, can explain murdering one of your employees, Lee Oswald, on television, then expecting people to believe some stranger just walked up to him in a police station and shot him in the gut? Blowing up buildings in downtown Manhattan and shooting a president in Dallas's Dealey Plaza are not fundamentally inexplicable moments, when some unpredictable event jars history and the whole world seems to tilt off its axis. They are moments of truth, where the national security state briefly shows itself. We don't want to believe it, but eventually the truth comes out, as it did for Bill Cosby.

For the most part, the national security state operates in secret. It prefers to do so. Occasionally it undertakes conspicuous, extraordinary actions where the risk of exposure exceeds what the state normally tolerates. Some extraordinary aim forces – or induces – it to act in public. The plotters of these crimes expect, from citizens' past behavior, that the Cosby rape principle protects them: charges of complicity become suppressed rumors because people do not want to believe them. The Cosby rape principle has another side to it, though. Eventually, people do believe the truth. Hannibal Burress chides Cosby for his criminal behavior in his stage performance. Someone in the audience posts a smartphone video on YouTube. The Internet goes crazy. Victim after victim comes out, encouraged because others suffered as they did. Suddenly that smug Cosby smile in the old photographs, and the devilish look in good ol' Bill's eye don't look so cute.

Eventually people understand that fire does not destroy steel-framed skyscrapers. They understand that the fatal wound to Kennedy's head did not result from a bullet that entered from the rear. Lastly, they understand that people they trusted are actually their enemies.

This transformation of beliefs suggests we analyze Kennedy's murder, and the attacks that occurred on 9/11. Analysis like that points to grounds for true belief in a political context. One way to approach the analysis is to consider what shapes political opinions. Another way is to ask how we distinguish truth from untruth in politics. A third question combines the first two: how do we sort true beliefs from opinion, and other kinds of beliefs we might hold in the political sphere? Laboratory scientists develop fairly sophisticated methods to sort what we know from what we do not, as they investigate all kinds of questions. People who seek knowledge about the political world cannot apply strictly experimental methods to the questions they investigate. Nevertheless, they do examine evidence and test hypotheses, so scientific methods are not entirely irrelevant.

We know that both crimes – Kennedy's murder and the events of 9/11 – have generated monumental disagreements about who committed these crimes, and how the perpetrators executed them. These disagreements point to differing standards of truth and methods of investigation. When you observe conflict this fundamental, where people disagree not only about what happened, but also about how to reach judgments in the matter, you know you have an interesting problem. You have crimes that call for some careful thought.

Infamy does not resolve these disagreements about standards and methods. It does open questions about how we solve political crimes, and how we do so when we do not have direct access to evidence. When we cannot evaluate evidence ourselves, our foremost way to make judgments efficiently is to decide which authorities we trust, and which we do not. We have to do that in numerous areas, especially for political crimes, because for most cases, we cannot possibly conduct our own primary research, engage in trial and error tests, conduct experiments, interview witnesses, observe events that have already occurred, examine crime scenes first-hand, or even read reliable accounts of the crimes. Everything we might do to find truth, without relying on authorities we trust, requires inordinate amounts of time. Except for our own areas of expertise, where people pay us to learn and develop knowledge, we must rely on authorities.

That creates a difficult set of issues for political knowledge, for the heavyweight authority in politics is government. Aside from its legal authority and monopoly on use of force, a fair number of citizens simply trust what political leaders and government officials say or write. Naturally that's not true for everyone, but we are raised, from the earliest years, to trust the people we obey. If you obey your parents at home and your teachers at school, you obey the law when you become an adult. Our social instincts teach that we submit to these authorities for our own protection. All of these authorities – parents, teachers, government officials – would not be authorities if you did not trust them. So by habit, we trust what they say, even if what they say is not in the nature of a command. If we can't trust the people who protect and care for us, then we truly inhabit a pitiless wilderness.

This habitual response to public authority may be misplaced. Let's say we set aside our faith in government's goodwill, and look at political crimes with the opposite presumption. Suppose we set aside government's account of these crimes at the start, because we suspect that anything government officials say is self serving and therefore not trustworthy. We might be wrong about that presumption from time to time, but we can bring official accounts into consideration later, if we find reasons to do that. If we are strict about this matter, we should not privilege those accounts, or even suggest they call for a response. To sort information efficiently, no type of evidence should take precedence over other types. If we must rely on authorities for reasons cited above – lack of time or opportunity to conduct original research – we ought to place government officials lowest on the list of authoritative sources. In fact, government officials place themselves there, through their own record of incompetent and misleading investigations.

If we conduct criminal and political inquiries in this way, so as to discount the authorities responsible for those investigations, we undertake something quite radical. We can easily find ourselves in a position where we question everything, and where no foundation furnishes a place to stand. We know that functioning without any kind of framework for our beliefs is psychologically untenable – and we instinctively stay away from it. Nevertheless, we should examine the habits that reinforce these instincts for stability. We habituate ourselves to paying serious attention to reports that bear a government seal. These reports bear the imprimatur of people like the chief justice of the Supreme Court. The chief justice presents his report to the president in a formal ceremony, with photographers present to record the ritual. Expert researchers write the reports. They contain findings. They compile and analyze far more evidence than we could ever gather ourselves. More than that, we pay for those reports. Do we want to say they are worthless, after all that?

If we want the truth, then we have to answer yes. Saying we want the truth, however, is not itself such a self-evident presupposition. A lot of people might honestly say, no thank you, we don't actually want the truth. The truth is kind of difficult to bear, it's destructive, it's troublesome, and it's unpredictable. The last thing you want, if you're comfortable and want to stay that way, is the truth. You'd be right about all those things. If you want comfort, then a government report that appears true is just the thing. As C. S. Lewis wrote, ""For what you see depends a good deal on where you are standing: it also depends on what sort of person you are."

Nevertheless if you want to solve a crime, you solve it, no matter where the evidence leads. Jim Garrison famously quoted the Latin legal principle, "Let justice be done though the heavens fall." When the heavens fall, discomfort ensues. Garrison's determination describes the calamity that may result when you seek the truth, but from Oedipus's son till this day, that's the nature of all inquiry. You can't know, when you start, what the outcome will be, where you'll wind up, or what consequences you'll suffer. You just have to trust, from beginning to end, that the truth yields a better outcome than untruth.

Motivations

People looked at the wreckage in New York, Pennsylvania, and the District of Columbia on September 12, 2001, and said, "9/11 changed everything." What the phrase meant at the time, however, is not what it turned out to mean later. At the time, people meant that we could not feel safe from the world anymore. We were at war, and our enemies could strike anywhere. They could annihilate thousands of people in downtown Manhattan. Homeland security became a national preoccupation.

Then, as many people around the world and in the United States began to realize what actually happened on 9/11, they began to see the calamity – and the putative initiation of hostilities – in a different way. They began to ask questions that the American government should have been able to answer, and could not. Gradually it became clear that government preferred not to answer straightforward questions because it had a lot to hide. At last, government officials refused to answer persistent and pointed questions from victims' families, because it could no longer hide what had become obvious: government counted itself among our enemies. 9/11 changed everything, because at last citizens perceived the truth about their own government.

Use of force to protect power

One article of faith for many Americans before 9/11 was that, for all its faults, our government was different from other governments. It did not routinely commit crimes against its own people. It tried to set an example of good behavior for other states. As a result, other states looked to it for leadership, and it responded generously. Among the things that changed on 9/11, this exceptional behavior and exceptional position were the first to go. The U. S. government became, in its own eyes and for others as well, just another powerful, illegal enterprise that served its own interests, not anyone else's. This change did not take place in one day, of course. The events that unfolded after 9/11, however, simply made these changes apparent to anyone who cared to observe them.

To see the direction of these changes, as well as their ominous outcomes should they go unchecked, consider the civil war in Syria. Not long after we unleashed the furies of armed conflict in Iraq, Jordan's King Abdullah worried that the war could spread to other countries in the region. His fears about contagion proved correct. We have seen prolonged civil conflict in Tunisia, Libya, Egypt, Syria, and Iraq. Syria's war is the most serious right now. It has already merged with the one in Iraq.

When we tote up the war crimes of the gang of cronies in Damascus, we see what a government will do to preserve its power. Is Syria an extreme case? Yes, it is, but our government has not bombarded cities, sniped citizens in the streets, or openly tortured children because it has not needed to. Given what it has already done, we cannot predict how much further it might go. As we assess the self protective actions of governments everywhere, we observe differences of degree, not kind. The more rulers feel threatened, the more force they employ. The more force they call into play, the more they undermine their ability to govern.

No one has charged the United States government with torture and murder of children, as Bashir Assad's government has done. Yet who predicted in the years after 9/11 that we would torture people on a large scale, and publicly defend these crimes? Moral decay occurs gradually, as does escalation in the use of violence. Assad's forces use their murderous techniques as means of intimidation: if we are willing to torture and kill this innocent young man, imagine what we will do to your family. Imagine what we will do to you.

Our government uses methods of intimidation, but it has not escalated its use of force against people to the degree we see in countries like Syria and Russia. As it feels itself under threat, however, it applies force sufficient to protect its power. No one can say, right now, what limits our government might observe to constrain its use of force. Rulers and secret police, for their part, like to create uncertainty on that score. Unpredictability and secrecy are hallmarks of people who operate outside the law.

Post-9/11 political dilemmas

Altogether, government's use of force and deception to protect its power and privileges presents something of a mystery. Before September 11, Richard Cheney's vulcans had all the power and prestige anyone could want, but it wasn't enough. They thought a new Pearl Harbor would establish our empire even more firmly. Now everyone can see that post-9/11 projection of power presents an entirely different mural of weakness and defeat. When the primary foundation for your power overseas is punishment, incompetent conquest and pusillanimous threats, you have already lost. Domestically, officials decked out in flag pins rule as a gang of cronies and criminals, protected by laws they promulgate or rescind to serve their own needs. They only pretend to lead. The pretense is part of their power.

So we ask, for tyrants everywhere who pretend to exercise leadership when their actual aims are much more exploitative: why do it? A government that has to use brutal methods has lost its legitimacy. It does not lead, nor can it accomplish any good for the country. The citizens know it and the government knows it. So what is the point of acting in a way that all – victims, bystanders, and perpetrators – recognize as destructive? We know the answer by now. Legitimacy, leadership, or serving citizens' welfare does not concern the government at all. Preservation of power – and continuance of the parasitic relationship where so-called public servants benefit from their access to the nation's treasury – is all that is at issue in this case. No one in Washington even pretends otherwise anymore.

Interestingly, our whole political culture has moved in a similar direction in the United States. We still have officials who praise public service, but even when they mean it, the praise sounds hollow. One travesty after another reminds us of the true relationship between government, and the people who suffer under its humiliations. As Peggy Noonan remarked about a wasteful government conference and shindig in Las Vegas, the notable thing was not that government officials wasted taxpayer money. That is not news. The notable thing is that they wasted taxpayer money, and openly mocked taxpayers while they did it.

So we understand that government officials not only feel entitled to throw a big party for themselves, but show contempt for the people who pay for it. As people remarked after seeing *Hunger Games*, someone needs to shoot the apple out of this pig's mouth. We need a leader who can make these jerks feel uneasy. We need a leader who demonstrates courage to say, "We will bring you down. You appropriated our republic for yourselves. We want it back." That would make their chests tighten up a bit. People who instill fear and humiliation in others, ought to feel a taste of it themselves.

Some would go further and say, "We will bring you down. We will put you away, as you put Jack and Bobby away." The problem is, the people who put Jack and Bobby away required only a few loaded guns and assassins to do so. You cannot replace your government with a few loaded guns. You cannot replace your government with a republic even if you have a lot of loaded guns. You have to find a way to remove government's internal supports. Think of a building, like World Trade Center 7, or a tent that collapses when you remove the supports that hold it up. A government's structural supports are financial and moral. Remove those, and the whole structure comes down.

"But we can't replace the government with anarchy," you say. Some would counter that anarchy, or something close to it, is the best possible outcome. Others would say our traditions call for more legal authority than anarchy would permit. That's why planning for a democratic republic, or multiple republics, must occur while the existing government, its wits clouded by its own power, prepares its own end. We know from history that when governments collapse, they collapse suddenly. They fall after an extended period of changes that throw it off balance, until it passes its tipping point. When we citizens observe government's self-destructive behavior, we have to recognize it. We have to be prepared to act when corrupt institutions at last inflict a blow, intended for their adversaries, that turns out to be fatal for them.

Path of self-destruction

The first, critical step onto this path of self-destruction occurred when hired assassins shot John Kennedy and John Connally in Dallas, Texas. The gunmen hit Connally by mistake. They executed President Kennedy in the nation's most infamous public square, Dealey Plaza. In most circumstances – think of Cesar Borgia in Machiavelli's *The Prince*, or Mexico's drug lords – the perpetrators of a murder like that would want people to know who did it. You can't intimidate and control people when you finger a fall guy to take the blame for your crimes.

The people who hit Kennedy wanted it both ways. They wanted a public execution, but they also wanted to keep who did it a secret. The CIA trained covert assassination teams to kill Fidel Castro, and murder was in the air. Their enemy in Havana might have been out of reach, but their enemy in Dallas was not. After Robert Kennedy received news of his brother's death, one of the first calls he made was to one of his contacts in the get-Castro underground. He asked right off the bat, "It was one of your guys, wasn't it?"

If we don't recognize the murder as an execution, we won't grasp its significance. If we don't grasp its significance, we won't be ready when the shadow state that planned this act reaches an endgame where its previous moves cause its own defeat. No government persists indefinitely after it squanders its legitimacy, just as no building can stand after its foundation explodes. Processes of institutional degradation and collapse may take some time; eventually a crisis or explosion occurs that reduces the weakened structure to a pile of bricks, shattered wood, or institutional chaos. Our government will not escape the destination it set for itself.

Already, our government displays every self-destructive behavior that governments headed for disaster have always displayed. It starts wars it cannot win. It borrows money it cannot repay to finance the wars. It confiscates money from its citizens to pay its debts. It acts above the law, under no constraints. It speaks arrogantly to other countries. It turns into itself, unable to set an example of leadership. Government becomes a parasite, and a vicious one at that.

Be ready

We citizens cannot resign, or become spectators in this process. If we merely watch, we could sit in bleachers, or in a prison camp that stretches from sea to sea, for two centuries or more. The Roman republic ended long before the structure fell. The secular power of the Catholic church in the Middle Ages underwent a similarly long decline. We still have enough freedom to prevent passive subjugation to corrupt tyrants and their toadies, who expect us to kiss their rings. We have to be ready for the crisis. We have to expect the explosion of civic energy that accompanies reform and revolution. We have to resist, plan, and rebuild, as the bloated ticks eventually fall off the unfortunate animal.

First, we have to resist government's overreach wherever we can. Our government maintains its power at our expense. It makes our lives miserable by degrees, so gradually that we don't realize how little freedom we have, or how much prosperity we have lost. We must find practical ways to resist processes of governmental aggrandizement, to regain our freedom, our elemental ability to act. We have become hamstrung. Freedom, which we all seek, includes capability to do work we love, and to dispose of our property as we wish. That yields happiness in social and economic enterprise. When government persistently interferes with citizens' pursuit of happiness, it violates every tenet of its own support.

Second, we have to plan to cooperate effectively. Carlos Casteneda wrote, "We either make ourselves miserable, or we make ourselves strong. The amount of work is the same." Collaboration to set plans of resistance, to execute strategies and guide civil action, is hard work. However difficult or risky, that work is better than the despair-inducing drudgery and indignity we suffer when we simply submit. We can act together to make our lives better, and to make our politics better as well.

Third, we have to prepare and build new institutions to replace decadent ones when they fall away. We know the dispiriting consequences of surprise, born of limited foresight: long periods of disorganized conflict, where powerful people willing to use the most force prevail, only to fall when a stronger person arrives. New rulers, flush with new power, may scheme more ruthlessly and energetically than the ones they replace. Powerful groups may put forward weak, incompetent stooges, who become no less criminal than their masters. Only citizens prepared to act in advance can prevent outcomes like that. Only prepared citizens can block or reverse the intimidation of secret police, the casual corruption of Rasputins and strongmen who pretend to be leaders, but behave as nothing more than party hacks and snakes who happen to have gained power.

Eventually the pot boils. Stay hungry. Be ready.

Make the Evidence Fit the Crime

Arlen "Make-the-evidence-fit-the-crime" Specter died in October 2012, at 82. People will praise his long service in the Senate. They'll speak admiringly about his toughness and his independence. They will mention his service as assistant counsel on the Warren Commission in 1964, but they won't dwell on it.

They should dwell on it. His tenure on the Warren Commission lasted only about nine months. What a significant nine months, though. During that time, Specter authored and supported the Commission's single bullet theory. It became the linchpin for everything else in the Commission's controversial report.

Single bullet theory

In a way, it's not fair to take Specter to task for this theory. If he had not developed it, someone else would have. That is, someone else would have had to do it. The charge from President Lyndon Johnson was clear: give me a report that validates the FBI's conclusions and evidence. The FBI decided within twenty-four hours of Kennedy's death that Lee Oswald shot the president, and that he acted alone. Specter's single bullet proposal gave Johnson what he wanted. The idea that one bullet caused multiple wounds to both Kennedy and Connally is the only theory that validates the FBI's conclusions.

The single bullet theory holds that a bullet from Oswald's rifle hit Kennedy in the back, emerged from his throat, then tumbled so as to cause multiple wounds to John Connally, who sat in front of Kennedy. If the Commission did not put forth this theory, it could not conclude that Oswald was the only shooter. Given the FBI's initial investigation of what happened in Dallas, the single bullet theory, and only this theory, ruled out multiple shooters.

A good deal of evidence indicates that Specter's theory is incorrect. Abraham Zapruder's films shows that Connally is not hit until after Kennedy is shot in the back: at least three seconds later, in fact. The doctors at Parkland hospital in Dallas agreed that a bullet entered Kennedy's throat from the front. Bob Harris's forensic analysis shows that Arlen Specter's single bullet could not have followed the path that the Warren Commission said it did.

I imagine President Johnson and others were grateful for Specter's ability to construct a halfway plausible theory, or more to the point, his willingness to stand by such an implausible one. If you wanted to believe the Warren Commission's report, you could hang your holster on the single bullet theory. If you found the entire report implausible, you would find little to admire in Specter's theory, too. The single bullet theory became the kernel at the heart of the Commission's report, the keystone of the FBI's package of conclusions and evidence. Take it or leave it.

Specter died forty-eight years and a month after the Commission released its report in September 1964. Specter was 34 at the time. I wonder if he proposed his theory as an act opportunism – please the boss to see where that will take you – or if he actually believed what he wrote. If he's like most of us, necessity convinced him of its truth. Of all people, Specter knew the necessary outcome of his investigation.

You could ask why a smart guy like Specter would have conceived a plainly implausible theory, inconsistent with virtually all the evidence available. Another question presses even more urgently. Who could have redirected the Commission's report, so it might be based on an actual investigation and honest evidence? The answer to that is simple: no one who worked for the president could do that. Johnson would get what he wanted. In light of the president's illicit demand for dishonesty, Specter served his president well. The Warren Commission could not have accomplished its mission without him.

Control crime scenes to clear evidence

Recall commentary in the United States after the crash of Malaysian Airlines Flight 17 in eastern Ukraine on July 16, 2014. Western observers made these points, with some urgency:

- We have to secure the crash scene. Put yellow crime tape around it. Don't leave it in control of Russian separatists, who control it now. They are the ones suspected of launching the missile that brought the plane down, so they have all incentive to hide and destroy evidence of what happened.

- We have to allow access by impartial investigators. That's not easy, in a war zone, but we have to do it. Only impartial investigators, not Russian separatists and their allies in Moscow, can learn exactly how this plane crash occurred.

- Thirdly, we want to treat the crash scene with respect. We don't want looting or tardy removal of bodies. We should return remains of the dead to their families as soon as we can.

These points are instructive because they take us to the period after September 11, 2001, when Europe and the rest of the world so hoped we – someone – would conduct a proper investigation of the attacks that occurred that day. Instead, the United States government declined to conduct any investigation at all. American authorities secured the crash scenes in Manhattan, Shanksville, Pennsylvania, and Washington, DC, not in order to gather and evaluate evidence, but to clear the evidence away as quickly as possible.

Consider the attack on the Pentagon, for example. Every crime scene investigator will say, the first rule is to leave everything exactly where it is, for investigators need to map out pieces of the plane, location of bodies, gather samples for laboratory testing, and so on. Instead, people from the FBI, the very agency we expected would conduct an investigation, cleared away evidence from the Pentagon attack as quickly as they could. The same story, on a larger scale, occurred in Manhattan. Authorities scooped up steel from the Twin Towers and shipped it overseas as expeditiously as they could. Shanksville tells the same story: secure the crash scene not to investigate it, but to clear away evidence so no one can investigate it.

So it goes when people want to hide the truth. The people who fired on Flight 17 near Donetsk bragged about bringing down a Ukrainian military transport plane. They actually posted a video – look what we did! – until they discovered their actual target had been a civilian airliner. Then they deleted evidence of their careless wartime   act immediately. When you launch a surface-to-air missile at a civilian aircraft by mistake, you don't apologize. You remove the evidence. The Russians have already blamed the Ukrainians for bringing down the airliner. Now they must destroy all evidence that contradicts the accusation.

After 9/11, those who controlled all three crime scenes had to cover their guilt. The same has already happened with the people who brought down Flight 17 over Ukraine. The mobile missile launcher is gone. Investigators say you have to leave the scene intact. Otherwise the evidence cannot reveal the truth. When you clean up the scene as fast as possible, as Johnson did with Kennedy's limousine, you cannot retrieve the stuff you washed away, removed, and destroyed. More recently, after the Germanwings crash in the French Alps, investigators treated the crash scene with care. They found the voice recorder, and quickly publicized the truth about why the crash happened.

In 2001, a shocked American public largely accepted the government's account of what happened on September 11. People in Europe were more skeptical. They would have liked to see a real investigation. By the time President Bush acceded to pressure, and created the 9/11 Commission in 2002, the evidence at all three locations was long gone. With no crime scene evidence to analyze, the commission instead wrote a treatise about how to prevent future attacks, and of course about the dangers posed by groups like Al Qaeda. The commission did not do any of the things you would expect an investigative commission to do. It couldn't. The evidence investigators need to analyze to determine what happened was gone.

So when we call for an impartial, international investigation of what happened in eastern Ukraine on July 16, 2014, we can think of a season, not so many years ago, when the rest of the world wanted to see a similar level of openness here in the United States. We know that Russia followed our example from 2001, not our words admonishment in 2014k, when they decided what to do about an investigation of the crash scene in Ukraine.

Russian security forces maintained control of the crash scene until the evidence was gone. In the short run, not coming clean always appears less costly than its opposite, telling the truth. In the long run, officials who want to hide their complicity in something bad – like shooting down an airliner or blowing up a skyscraper – don't think that distrust from people they don't see, and never will see, is all that high a price to pay. They just don't want to be caught out. If you want to hide your complicity and guilt, you must remove and destroy evidence of that guilt. This pattern of concealment has become so common that we do not expect honest from public officials any longer. We used to call it, euphemistically, the credibility gap. Now this kind of public dishonesty is taken for granted. Trust ought to bind leaders to their followers, but if you have a lot to hide, trust is the last thing on your mind.

Good enough for government work

"It's good enough for government work," people used to say when I served in the Navy. Commonly spoken to wrap up a job, you might say it was the government's version of the 80/20 rule: stop when you're eighty percent done, because the last twenty percent isn't worth it. In practice, it means we hold government work to a lower standard of quality when we evaluate it. Oddly, we don't expect much from government employees, no matter what their level.

Now we have to ask whether this kind of thinking holds when the government undertakes cover-ups. When Lyndon Johnson decided he needed Chief Justice Earl Warren to write a report on President Kennedy's assassination, did he expect the commission to apply the good enough standard? Did Johnson think that Warren's high office and authority would take care of that extra twenty percent? After all, if you plan to lay out your case against

Lee Oswald, you don't want to put out a shoddy, incomplete piece of work and hope it will fly. A large dash of prestige makes the product more persuasive.

Few expected the Warren report to silence people who were already skeptical of the government's story. Johnson launched the commission's investigation to quell doubts among everyone else, to make sure the skeptics did not gain an advantage over time. Fifty years later, the Warren Commission's work appears to have accomplished its purpose, for a generation anyway. It kept the initial gaggle of conspiracy nuts at bay. It also demonstrated that even when the stakes could not be higher for an investigation, government's habit of mediocrity reliably accompanies – and then undermines – its own deceit, no matter how prestigious or capable the author. Even as a cover-up, the Warren Commission report did a poor job.

By comparison with the Warren Commission report, was the 9/11 Commission report good enough to accomplish its purpose? Consider these points related to the 9/11 Commission's success or failure: (1) the Bush administration obstructed formation of the commission for two years, so fresh evidence had a long time to dissipate; (2) the differences between what witnesses saw, heard and recorded photographically, and what people read in the report were enormous; (3) after the Kennedy assassination and Warren report, Americans did not want to be hoodwinked again.

Another interesting comparison between the JFK and 9/11 investigations exists. The Warren Commission assembled some twenty-three volumes of testimony, whereas the 9/11 Commission relied on fake computer simulations. We know that you can make computer simulations come out any way you like. Both commissions aimed to construct and explicate a preset narrative. For the Warren report, though, all those volumes of testimony made its evidence and conclusions appear more weighty.

Weighty or not, the 9/11 Commission's report appears to be less persuasive than the Warren Commission report. How many years passed before the majority of Americans came to doubt the government's version of Kennedy's assassination? Collective judgments about the government's version of 9/11 required a lot less time to reach that threshold. In both cases, a written report produced by men of prestige made the government's version more persuasive. In both cases, the plainly fraudulent character of each report became apparent over time. They were fraudulent because each one became a huge exercise in misdirection. Despite the high standing of the authors, each report failed even the modest standard of mediocrity set for government work.

As we look at the aftermath of each crime, however, particularly the consolidation of federal power and autonomy, the modest standard of good enough seems to hold. You can fool quite a few people for a while. The criminals who planned these attacks relied on that general rule to get by. Though the crimes were not perfect – certainly not executed well enough to conceal their true origins – they were, for their time, good enough to accomplish their aims, and good enough to free their perpetrators from fear of punishment.

The criminals who planned Kennedy's murder executed a coup d'état. Thirty-eight years later, the criminals who planned the 9/11 attacks decisively advanced our nation's transformation from a constitutional republic with limited powers to something far more ominous. These two crimes – bold and psychologically effective – were clearly good enough for government work.

Mass Psychosis and Interpretation of Evidence

Do you know what the term *mass psychosis* means to a psychologist, a sociologist or a psychiatrist? I'm sure those specialists debate its causes and effects quite a bit. When those arguments filter into the mainstream, do we comprehend what they are talking about? Or is mass psychosis one of those constructs that's so attractive because no one knows what it means? Let's consider a plain language understanding of the term, as it applies to 9/11 and other social trauma. Let's see where the inquiry leads.

What's the first thing that comes to your mind when you see the phrase mass psychosis? Lemmings running over a cliff, right? Orson Welles' *War of the Worlds* broadcast in 1938 might come to mind, too, or the Red Scare of the early 1950s if you think a little longer. You have the Salem witch trials if you go further back. Nazi party rallies at Nuremburg have to be on the list. Even Beatle mania might count if you include the fun and harmless. Few right now would recognize 9/11 as an example. Someday people will.

Before we develop this point a little, let me comment briefly on the initial phase of the 2003 war, Shock and Awe. I wonder sometimes why our Pentagon planners, or whoever they were, picked this phrase to describe a bombing campaign that targeted Iraqi cities. They might as well have picked a name like Guernica, to describe an operation to drop bombs on urban areas where many civilians live close together. That's why we remember Picasso's painting, or the statue in Rotterdam's city center, both memorials to the destruction and cruelty of aerial bombing.

What, in the end, is the difference between the bombing of Rotterdam at the beginning of World War II, and the destruction of Dresden a few years later? What is the difference between Pearl Harbor and the Rape of Nanjing on one side, and Hiroshima on the other? The difference, we readily say, is that the Germans and the Japanese started the war. They launched the wars in Europe and the Pacific. That's the moral difference, between aggressors and defenders.

We launched the war in Iraq with our attack on Baghdad. A name like Shock and Awe cannot disguise our moral position, cannot conceal our responsibility for the people who died in Baghdad, cannot distract anyone from what the United States actually did. We fought an aggressive war in Vietnam, but no full scale attack before Shock and Awe amounted to a blatant war crime. No attack on another country, except perhaps crimes we committed in the Philippines during the Spanish American war, was so clearly indefensible.

Why do you suppose our war planners and public relations people should have chosen Shock and Awe to promote their campaign of death? Why did they give their bombing campaign any name at all? Interestingly, they could have used Shock and Awe to describe the purpose and effects of the 9/11 attacks just eighteen months earlier. Those events occurred right here. Did they originate here as well? The official reply to that question amounts to: Wouldn't you like to know? Don't bother with questions like that. We have wars to fight, countries to conquer, cities to bomb, people to torture, tyrants to hang.

Thank God for video evidence

The idea of mass psychosis makes us see some interesting relations among perception, belief, and language. Via live television or first hand on September 11, or through video recording afterward, we see the destruction and say, "Look, that building exploded." Someone in authority arrives to say no, it collapsed due to gravity and structural damage. People who witnessed the explosions say, "Yes, yes, collapse." We don't want to contest the official account because someone might call us a whacko conspiracy nut. In fact, people who contest the official account are already called that.

In Life of Brian, the main character, mistaken for the messiah, gets exasperated because people follow him around. He tells his would-be followers, "Look, you can think for yourselves. You're all individuals." The crowd in front of him shouts back, in unison, "Yes, yes, we're all individuals." 9/11 is a good test for all of us: can we think for ourselves, or not? Can we think thoughts that might bring ridicule from our neighbors and friends? Fear of what others might think is a type of mass psychosis.

So let's take a brief look at the video evidence from 9/11. In the case of the Twin Towers, we see two 110 story buildings demolished from the top down. Any unprompted account of the matter would say the demolition occurred due to a rapid series of explosions. We cannot tell what causes the destructive release of energy. The explosions progress in sequence from the top of the tower to its base. The explosions destroy the building's frame, as well as the building materials the frame supports.

The third building to come down that day, World Trade Center 7, does indeed appear to collapse. It suffered no damage during the attacks that would impair the strength or integrity of its supporting columns. Whatever brought it down occurred inside the building – we do not see explosions outward as we do with the Twin Towers. World Trade Center 7 collapsed in about seven seconds. Everything about the collapse – everything – points toward a controlled demolition. No contradictory evidence supports an alternate explanation.

When you see a video recording of World Trade Center 7's collapse, you immediately think, "That's fishy. That didn't happen because office fires in the lower half of the building triggered a catastrophic collapse." That's the government's version. When your eyes tell you one thing and a government report tells you something else, which will you believe? Which authority carries more weight? As Ronald Reagan said a long time ago about someone who looked less than forthright on television: "The camera doesn't lie."

Laws of physics, laws of nature

People skeptical of government's explanation for the Twin Towers' collapse point to a simple principle of physics – conservation of energy – to underpin their questions. A system generally contains three types of energy: potential energy, kinetic energy, and thermal energy. All three types can perform work. Moreover, we can measure energy, both before and after it performs work.

Consider each tower as a system. It contains no kinetic energy unless it sways in high winds. The structure contains no thermal energy, except the warmth it absorbs from the sun. Almost all the energy in the system at rest is potential – the result of lifting large masses high above the ground. If the structure supports its own weight, it remains intact and stationary. Gravity is the only natural force that can convert the potential energy stored in such a system to kinetic energy.

Thermal energy is another matter. The government argues that burning aviation fuel added heat to the structure, causing it to fail where the structural damage was greatest. After that, gravity and a so-called zipper effect did the rest. The government's zipper-and-pancake theory says that a progressive, floor by floor failure caused the entire building to collapse. The only source of energy for this destruction was the potential energy stored in the structure, converted by the earth's gravitational field into kinetic energy as the building came down.

No part of this theory fits the visual evidence. We see the concrete in each tower turned to dust. We see steel beams blown out the side of each building, to land a couple of football fields away. We see all of that happen in about twelve seconds. Afterward we see vast pools of molten metal underneath the rubble, metal that remains liquid for weeks. That's conservation of energy. No physicist can explain to you how to convert the potential energy of a skyscraper in a gravitational field to molten metal.

No theory that relies only on aviation fuel and gravity can explain any of these phenomena. To overlook the existence of molten metal underneath the wreckage is the most extreme case of willful self-deception. Turning concrete to dust, throwing steel girders hundreds of yards – for both of these one might say, "Well, you had an awful lot of potential energy in those buildings." You can't say that about the molten metal. No amount of potential energy in the original structure can explain that.

Mass psychosis

That returns us to our original observation. What explains self-deception of this type, a willingness to disregard the evidence of our own eyes? What must happen after perception if we see one thing, and interpret it as something else? Psychologists love to analyze this problem, but it gets tricky when a large number of people in contact with one another fall into the same mistake. How do you explain an erroneous pattern of thought that replicates itself? To do so, we must bring together mental processes that occur in an individual brain, with social processes that occur in a much larger social organism.

Three well known processes come into play in a case like this: acceptance of authority, fear of ostracism, and discomfort with uncertainty.

Acceptance of authority. Many citizens trust the government. In fact, they regard public trust and obedience as marks of good citizenship, since government translates social norms into legal ones. In our families, we are trained to associate acceptance of authority with goodness. Likewise in our schools, we train students to obey the public authority they find outside their families. We all seek approval, and obedient students receive plenty of it. They know they are good boys and girls.

Fear of ostracism. Second, no one wants to be ridiculed or ostracized. That is perhaps the worst and most painful punishment the social organism can inflict on an individual: rejection to the point of isolation, until the individual in question feels entirely alone. That amounts to death, and in fact it often results in death.

Discomfort with uncertainty. Lastly, living with uncertainty about traumatic crimes and major loss quickly becomes disagreeable. We function best with routines and familiar beliefs. People need and seek a degree of certainty about their environment. That includes their mental and emotional states. If explanations about a crime offer to overturn a person's entire world view, because those explanations place responsibility for the crime in unimaginable places, that creates painful uncertainty. You can expect individuals to resolve questions like that as quickly as they can.

Interpretation of 9/11 evidence introduces questions that can undermine one's fundamental picture of the world. If one resolution of those questions points toward ostracism, disobedience, distrust and uncertainty, whereas another resolution points toward social acceptance and a degree of confidence about the essential qualities of one's environment, we can predict fairly well how many individuals resolve questions like that. Their first instinct will be, "I don't really want to think about that." If they do think about it, they will be sensitive to what other people think.

Once more on video evidence

I'm sure the people who planned Kennedy's murder would not wish that Abraham Zapruder had filmed the president's public execution. All the discussion about whether the government doctored the film misses this point: no amount of doctoring could disguise the backward snap of Kennedy's head, or Jackie's sudden movement to the limousine's trunk to retrieve a piece of her husband's brain tissue. No single shooter behind the car can account for what we see with our eyes in that film.

When you add the evidence in the film to Jack Ruby's murder of Lee Oswald on live television two days later, you create a huge fishiness factor. No matter what *Life* magazine tells you, a large number of people will think, "What's going on here?" Yet the social phenomena we've discussed make many reluctant to talk about their doubts with family and friends. Fifty years later, we're more open to talking about it. This week, Robert Kennedy Jr. said that his dad thought the Warren report was "a shoddy piece of craftsmanship." The day his brother died, Robert Kennedy did not believe Lee Oswald acted on his own. His son Robert Kenney Jr. does not believe it now.

The same kind of thing will happen – has already started to happen – with 9/11. Right now, skeptics who say, "Look what's right in front of your eyes," meet substantial resistance. If they become well known, or pose a genuine threat, they can encounter more than that. Consider Mary Meyer, Jack Kennedy's lover, shot to death near a canal in Washington DC because her enemies feared what she might say about his death. Courageous people who speak publicly against the government's account of 9/11 – people like David Ray Griffin – know what happened to Mary Meyer.

Forty or fifty years from today, the social environment will have changed. The people who actually demolished the World Trade Center buildings will not be alive. If we still have a democracy, people will talk more freely about the event. Today we talk more freely about Kennedy's assassination, two generations after the events in Dallas. Evidence collected and analyzed so long after the fact may be less conclusive than evidence collected on the spot, but it is still valuable. Moreover, analysts have a larger framework of evidence available after time has passed. As a result, pieces of evidence – and the conclusions they yield – become less fragmentary. Even more importantly, as analysts correlate pieces in a growing field of interpretation, they advance the good work that precedes theirs.

Reprise on psychosis

Psychosis sounds so painful, so weighty and so out there. We don't like to think about mental illness, for some of the same social reasons we've discussed. Mentally ill people become ostracized, placed physically apart from the rest of us. All of us experience problems with our mental and emotional health. Not one of us wants to spend time in a sanitarium, a place apart. If questions of psychosis arise in a personal way, we'd like to change the subject. It's the last thing we care to think about.

Yet psychosis merely refers to an unhealthy state of mind. If we deny the truth or the evidence of our own eyes because we have an unhealthy state of mind, we should try to do something about that. Individuals can respond as they wish to various states of mind – that's part of what we mean by individual freedom. If as a collective body – a social organism – we find problems related to states of mind, we ought to address those, together. Some types of benign self-deception help us get through life. We can't deny the truth about 9/11, however, and hope that the results are good for us. They won't be.

Who Fills the Well First?

If you have not yet read James Douglass's *JFK and the Unspeakable: Why He Died and Why It Matters*, do so. To see why I recommend Douglass's book, read the first chapter in this book. For an easier read that complements *JFK and the Unspeakable*, read David Talbot's *Brothers*. Both books, published in 2008, are worth your time. Both books present a view of the Kennedy years not available during the 1960s or, for that matter, any other decade before they were published.

The mathematician and philosopher Laplace said that "the weight of evidence for an extraordinary claim must be proportioned to its strangeness." That leaves to individual judgment whether or not one regards something as strange. Some might think the idea that Kennedy died for political reasons extraordinary, where others would regard a politically motivated assassination as entirely normal. Put briefly, the latter view holds there's nothing extraordinary about political assassination.

Political leaders throughout history, if they have enemies, bet their lives. Almost all political leaders have enemies. They know that if things do not go the right way – if something goes amiss or they commit a serious error – they may be executed, assassinated, exiled, or removed from office in disgrace. People who operate in the political arena play for keeps. Political killings stand out in history not because they are rare, but because they spawn significant consequences. Historians often tie them to a characteristic type of political disintegration.

James Douglass's account of Kennedy's death only appears extraordinary because the Warren Commission had the first lick. The Commission's report became the first widely accepted explanation of Kennedy's death. It encompassed twenty-six volumes of carefully catalogued testimony and evidence. The chief justice of the Supreme Court blessed it. President Johnson accepted it at a presentation ceremony and photo opportunity. It had the seal of the United States government on its cover, just like the 9/11 Commission report. No wonder so many people at the time trusted its veracity.

If Douglass had published his account first, and prominent people had blessed his research, the idea that Lee Oswald killed Kennedy by himself would seem extraordinary. During the traumatic hours immediately after the murder, however, officials managed to fix Oswald's guilt in people's minds. Delivering the first apparently credible package of information confers a large advantage in this kind of situation. Because the official narrative influences perceptions and memories, because it defines the boundaries of acceptable belief, the early accounts shape political and social reality. You can recover from these presumptions and rhetorical disadvantages if you disbelieve the official account, but effective rebuttal requires considerable work.

Example from electoral politics

Think about another interesting example in political life of a weighty blow delivered first. On election night in 2000, the first unofficial tally in Florida had Bush ahead by about five hundred votes. On that basis, Tom Brokaw, and a few others, called the election for Bush. The over-eager reporters embarrassed themselves. Florida's results in 2000 proved just as close as results for the 2008 Franken-Coleman Senate race in Minnesota. That is, the Florida vote was essentially a tie: the state had to organize and execute a legal – and political – process to determine the winner, as did Minnesota eight years later.

The Supreme Court said we could not wait around for Florida's legal process. It declared a winner. Its only conceivable basis for declaring Bush the winner was that Bush went to bed on election night with Tom Brokaw blessing his victory. When he needed a good team of lawyers to assert that Tom Brokaw was correct, he had that, too. If Tom Brokaw had declared Gore the winner on election night, no one imagines the Supreme Court would have appointed Bush to the White House. Bush's Florida tally, together with NBC's strange, statistically perverse decision to declare the winner before everyone went to bed, set a course for everything that happened afterward. Bush and Brokaw got in the first licks.

The Kennedy case

To form judgments and narratives about the troubling events in Dallas, the FBI, the Dallas police and the Dallas district attorney came in first. The Warren Commission confirmed and gave formal shape to the early accounts. After that, opposing accounts seemed unreasonable and unwelcome, out of the mainstream, kooky, counter-productive, and suspect. The conspiracy theorists are at it again, people thought. Jim Garrison and the others should let it go. The assassination researchers appeared suspect not because they were wrong, or because their evidence was inferior to the government's evidence, but because they came in second.

When we compare the methods, logic, and evidence in the Warren Report to the methods, logic, and evidence of competing accounts, the alternate versions look more reasonable straight down the line. To take one key instance, Arlen Specter's single-bullet theory, articulated in the Warren Report to account for the ballistic evidence, is so utterly fantastic, so disconnected from other evidence, that every other explanation of what occurred inside and outside Kennedy's car appears superior. If Douglass's book had appeared in 1964, and the Warren Report had appeared in 2008, comparisons of quality would be no contest at all. Every careful reader would judge Douglass's account superior.

Template-based state crimes

A template-based, state crime has three qualities: it is based on a plan, standard procedures enable a sizable organization to execute the plan, and lastly, procedures must include concealment of evidence and misdirection to protect perpetrators and others. The third characteristic concerns assembly of an early, official narrative plausible enough to garner belief from people inclined to credit reports from people in positions of authority. Concealment of evidence and misdirection – think of the adept street performer who entertains with "magic" tricks – are central to these latter procedures.

When we compare JFK's murder with 9/11 and other state crimes against democracy, we find these common practices on the part of state authorities: (1) control the crime scene, to clean it up as quickly as you can; (2) identify the culprit quickly; (3) develop a narrative that is not too specific about the evidence; (4) suppress alternate theories of the crime; (5) destroy, conceal, or discredit evidence that supports alternate theories.

Because government organizations must rely on these techniques, and because these techniques are often inconsistent with standard procedures, use of these methods often indicates something amiss. State authorities will try to use standard procedures no matter who committed a crime, but the way they behave after a crime depends on whether they want to convict an actual criminal, or protect people within their own organizations. If the latter, their execution of standard procedures lends itself to concealment or destruction of evidence, and direction of attention away from what actually happened.

September 11 narrative

Interestingly, George W. Bush chose not to follow Lyndon Johnson's precedent when he resisted formation of the 9/11 Commission. Cheney and Bush must have judged that the early accounts in *The New York Times* were good enough. The war planners in the White House clearly hoped pressure to launch a formal investigation would go away. When it heightened instead, the president signed legislation to form the commission in November 2002. It completed its work in August 2004, almost three years after the event.

By then, a number of 9/11 researchers had begun to publish their findings. Sober researchers described several anomalies, most notably the controlled demolition of World Trade Center Building 7. Other questions related to destruction of the Twin Towers, distribution of wreckage near Shanksville, Pennsylvania, the strange explosion at the Pentagon, odd behavior of the FAA and military air defense forces, cavalier treatment of crime scene evidence, and misinformation about the attackers, phone calls from the aircraft, audio evidence of explosions at the towers, implausibility of the official pancake theory, the president's and Secret Service's strange behavior during the attacks, and of course the rush to blame Osama bin Laden when no evidence of his involvement existed. Numerous anomalies, lacunae, oversights, contradictions and whoppers coalesced to indicate that official accounts of what happened on 9/11 were false.

In light of these developments, President Bush might have conceded first licks to multiple other researchers, had he not had super-compliant media to echo everything his government wanted to put out. From the first minutes and hours of the crisis, public media proved willing to serve up the government's line. Accounts of how World Trade Center 7 fell illustrate this phenomenon of compliance. So many people knew in advance this forty-seven story building would come down, that one news broadcast reported its destruction twenty minutes before it actually did come down! When it collapsed into its own footprint, the media uncritically repeated official government explanations, without independent investigation. The building fell due to fire and structural failure, no questions asked. The White House could not have asked for more. When you have people willing to report even obvious lies as the truth, you do not need a formal commission to certify your version. Media consensus and quiescence serve just as well.

Did the people who planned World Trade Center 7's demolition think we would not notice what happened? Perhaps they thought that seven hours after the twin towers exploded, we would not notice that a forty-seven story steel frame building imploded and fell straight down in seven seconds. They were almost right. In the climate of jingoistic fear that followed 9/11, people with guts had to point it out. They had to draw our attention to it, and demonstrate the significance of this controlled demolition in the framework of the day's events.

Skeptics say they want a smoking gun to prove wrongdoing, especially when we accuse our own government. For attorneys in court, smoking gun evidence is so fresh, material, and decisive that the other side cannot contest it. In World Trade Center 7, the perpetrators of the 9/11 crimes handed us a smoking gun. All the evidence for destruction of Building 7 indicates a controlled demolition. No evidence contradicts this assessment. Seldom does one event so conclusively demonstrate brazen deceit, evasion, and ill intent from people who lie to us.

Mockingbird

On February 27, 1968, Walter Cronkite declared during a television broadcast that the Vietnam war was not worth it. The effect of that statement on the country was unmistakable. People trusted his judgment, and had no reason to think he would say anything other than the truth. If he was a national father figure, he was also a national conscience. On March 31, thirty-two days after Cronkite rejected the president's leadership as commander in chief, Lyndon Johnson announced he would not run for reelection: an astonishing defeat for a corrupt but savvy politician.

Could anything like that happen nearly half a century later? Our media, and their audience, are more fragmented today. We do not, and will not again, have a single figure with Cronkite's influence. Nevertheless, imagine if The New York Times questioned the government's version of what happened on 9/11. Imagine if Ben Bradlee and the Washington Post had treated the Kennedy assassination as they treated Watergate. Would we even have terms like truther and conspiracy theorist floating around?

We would not. Substantial opinion around the country would openly align itself with respectable sources like these. Instead of wondering what people might say if they don't keep their mouths shut, skeptics might emerge from the weeds. Tables turned, people might not feel so comfortable about ridiculing critics who ask questions. People on both sides of these questions might respect the evidence more, and dishonest government officials less. We might even wonder about those odd people who find government reports trustworthy.

The difference in 1968 was that Walter Cronkite looked at the evidence, and evaluated it by his own lights. He had integrity. More than that, people knew he was honest. You cannot say that about today's media. They want to stay on government's good side, even though it does not have one. Prestige still swirls around power. Today's media want to be close to the purple, or as we would say now, close to the levers of power. What person in the mainstream media would not want to say at a dinner party, "I was talking to the president today, and…"?

Explanations for media compliance

Why do people in the media, so long after Cronkite's era, seem so willing to report the government's line? What leverage does the government have over them? Or does the explanation have little to do with overt leverage? Several explanations for apparent media compliance come to mind:

Inherent limitations. Reporters must produce a lot of copy with few resources, they work under deadline, and they like to tip back a beer with their colleagues now and then. To deal with these pressures and limits, work with public information lying close by.

Corporatism. The standard leftist view is that newspapers are owned by big corporations, big corporations are interested in big profits, and if you want to make a profit in this world, you need a friendly relationship with the government.

Inside information. Reporters obtain a lot of what seems like inside information from their sources in government. They don't want their flow of information to dry up if they publish stories critical of the institutions and sources that sustain them.

Patriotic sentiments and customs. Reporters, like people in their audience, often act from a sense of patriotism. Therefore they don't criticize their country in public, especially during wartime.

Special relationships. Reporters might have a relationship with the Central Intelligence Agency or other propaganda arm that obligates them to frame their reports on U. S. government activities in a certain way.

Servility. Reporters are impressed by people with power, and they want to suck up to people who have it.

Careerism. Journalists want to advance in their professions. The best way to do that is break big stories and be seen with the in crowd. The implications are obvious.

Fear of getting scooped. If you do not get the story first, someone else will. If someone else gets it first, you'll be seen as a loser. To be a winner, associate with other people who are winners.

State propaganda

Except for the first, all of these possibilities speak to the sociology of political information in a culture where the state is over-powerful, and therefore receives more attention and deference than it deserves. If key media outlets or individuals are in the government's pocket, or align themselves too closely with the state, it should not be hard to find evidence of that. The problem is, the outlets in the best position to find and publicize that evidence would never do it. Moreover, alternative media outlets most likely to report such evidence, if it exists, are not in a great position to find it, let alone report it.

One reason for thinking along these lines is Operation Mockingbird, a disturbing government operation of the 1950s and 1960s. When you learn the Washington Post and managing editor Ben Bradlee had a tight relationship with the CIA, you think, "Good God, is that what we have for the Fourth Branch of government? These supposed watchdogs actually work as cat's paws for the state?" When you learn that the newspaper of record for the nation's capital is nothing but a state organ, that gives you pause. No matter how cynical you are, you find you have not been cynical enough. No matter how disillusioned you become, the truth still finds a few more ideals to destroy.

The aptly named Operation Mockingbird was an effort to keep the United States press on government's side during the Cold War. Interestingly, not one news outlet, columnist or reporter has ever admitted to working with the CIA or other agency, nor have they apologized for it. Not one editor has acknowledged this kind of professional corruption. Without that acknowledgement, not one news organization has ever indicated that such a corrupt relationship has ended.

More and more, propaganda displays itself as an explicit part of our national life. We know it exists, but how can we determine where it originates? To start with, the state does not want you to know where it originates. As citizens who need to know about government's activities, we need access – and insight – to make judgments about how our news forms. In the current abundance of multi-platform media, we can only make judgments about the content in front of us. We can also compare that content with what we remember. If people who bring us that content have a relationship with government we should know about, let them tell us about it. In this case, people who create news in collaboration with the state know how to keep secrets almost as well as their masters.

State suppression

Consider a recent example of tacit compliance in the media. Reflect on its implications for public reporting about 9/11, Kennedy's murder, the Iraq war, and other crimes. Recall the way *The New York Times* reported on Bradley Manning: his act of resistance, his imprisonment, and his trial. WikiLeaks data from Manning's computer furnished the Times with a deep well of true information about U. S. activities abroad. The Times collaborated with WikiLeaks, used its documents freely, and improved its reporting as a consequence. Then the government brought its weighty hammer down on WikiLeaks, shut off its funding, maneuvered its leader Julian Assange into exile, and – with the United Kingdom's help – essentially turned a legitimate international enterprise into an outlaw organization.

As the feds undertook their plan to crush WikiLeaks, the Times' articles on Bradley Manning became markedly unsympathetic. After WikiLeaks was out of the picture, the Times ignored Manning's case altogether. Not only did the Times show no gratitude to Manning, it participated in his destruction as he disappeared into solitary confinement. If you wanted to find coverage of his trial, you had to read elsewhere. For the most part, editors at the Times ignored him and his cause.

What leverage could the government have used with the Times to induce such a noticeable and public betrayal? Does anyone doubt that if the government had not locked Manning away in a tiny cell twenty-three hours a day – had not humiliated him and treated him as a dangerous traitor – the Times would have treated him as anything but an honorable and even heroic revealer of government crimes in the middle of a horrific war founded on lies? Government can act this way only because Manning and other courageous whistleblowers have found no defenders at the Times, or at any other major news organization for that matter.

Bradley Manning's act of civil resistance is at least as significant as Daniel Ellsberg's publication of the Pentagon Papers in 1971, as Ellsberg himself testifies. After decades of giving Ellsberg the honor he deserves, the Times now treats both Manning and Ellsberg as if they did not exist. Apparently, government has created just the right atmosphere of caution, fear, intimidation, and collaboration at media organizations like the Times.

To see how we reached this point during decades of servility and special relationships between power people and those who report or interpret the news, read No Place to Hide by Glenn Greenwald. Greenwald, a journalist himself, helped Edward Snowden reveal crimes committed at the National Security Agency. In his online articles, Greenwald courageously and correctly criticizes his colleagues in journalism. He does not forgive them their compliance or their cowardice, and he is equally hard on their government handlers. Because relationships between press and power have become so close, corrupt and mutually dependent, we must seek truthful reporting somewhere else. We won't find independent, accurate information where dishonesty and an insider's mentality have taken root.

Concluding thought

A key principle of democratic government underlines these observations about media compliance. Without openness, integrity, and ready access to accurate information, citizens who oversee government cannot influence its activities or stop its crimes. Without independent media, government controls citizens. When authority flows downward from the powerful few to everyone else, you have an anti-democratic political structure. That is why democratic government depends on unencumbered, truthful information.

Under multiple cloaks of secrecy and dishonesty, the state protects itself. The cloaks only hide the worst of it. If the state lies and schemes and violates the law openly, what does it do in secret? Plenty, it turns out. Power generates excess, self-sustaining energy. People who seek that kind of power, or who believe in its beneficial effects, tend to be unskeptical about it. People detached from anti-democratic power, or who recognize its harmful effects, tend not to grant authorities benefit of the doubt for anything. They expect the worst. They observe what government does in plain sight, and begin to ask questions about things we cannot see. People who believe in the state's ability to work for the benefit of all cannot see why skeptics denigrate government's efforts at every turn.

These two views about government do not commingle readily. They incorporate drastically different conceptions of citizenship. At a certain point, these perspectives become irreconcilable, especially if key sources of information collaborate with the state. When that happens, no one trusts anyone. Gradually, media collaboration evolves into a loose form of state control, where media organizations realize their institutional norms no longer support independent journalism. When you observe the way journalists have treated questions surrounding 9/11, and compare that behavior to Walter Cronkite's report on the Vietnam war in 1968, you do start to doubt whether large media organizations exercise any independence at all.

The bin Laden Hit and Torture

What does public dishonesty signify? It might signify hypocrisy, intentional misdirection, or a desire to conceal truth to escape blame. Big lies begin small. At last propaganda, image making, concealment and garden variety lying become so habitual that perpetrators cannot distinguish reality from self-justification. When you cannot make rational judgments about the essential nature of your actions, let alone their legality, you may begin to behave, and talk, in ways that make people disbelieve you. We have had deeply, instinctively skeptical reactions so often now, we hardly care to think about them. When public dishonesty becomes that habitual, when telling the truth becomes an exceptional act, you know the public space has become corrupt.

You do not even need independent evidence to see that government's statements about its own actions do not square up. Its claims about its own activities are so inconsistent and laced with dishonesty that you wonder why they trouble themselves with this stuff. The example I have in mind here is the Osama bin Laden hit. Dishonesty about his killing is evident on two levels: statements about the act itself, and statements about how the act was possible. Let's address the act itself, then its precursors.

Assassination or self-defense?

First, let's consider official statements about the killing. Everything about the mission indicates it was a planned assassination. Given bin Laden's location deep inside Pakistan, any other plan increased the likelihood of failure. To reduce that likelihood, you send in a team of assassins, not a team of sheriffs who plan to bring their quarry in for questioning. Yet the government's statements afterwards pretended that bin Laden was shot because he tried to resist, he reached for his weapon, he or his guards did something or other that made the SEAL team plug him twice in the head.

That does not sound right. You went in there to take him prisoner, but you shot him twice in the head because he reached for a weapon? Why did spokesmen at the White House prevaricate about such a significant event? The mission's successful outcome, after all, warranted a presidential speech from the White House. What kept you from simply telling people what happened, consistent with the SEAL team's obvious intent?

Turns out the answer to that question is simple enough. States don't assassinate people. It violates domestic law to do it in your own country; it violates international law to do it in someone else's country. So even though you obviously assassinated someone – and in case anyone missed the point, you dumped the body in the ocean – you cannot call it an assassination. You pretend the hit was not a hit. You pretend the SEALs shot him in self defense, even though no one believes that, and few in the United States care much one way or another. The president said that we got him: justice was done.

Here is a puzzle about the assassination that I want to present without an excess of insinuation. Why did the White House reveal who carried out the killing? Could this revelation have been an inexplicable blunder, a misplaced desire to give credit to a secret hit team? If so, government must be just as bad at truth-telling as it is at lying. When the White House praised members of SEAL Team Six in public, members of the team knew immediately that they had become targets. At 02:38 on August 6, 2011, the Taliban brought down the team's Chinook helicopter just three months and four days after Osama bin Laden died on May 2. All thirty-eight people in the helicopter died.

What is the purpose of so-called harsh interrogation methods?

The second point concerns information that let SEAL Team Six locate bin Laden. Apologists for the CIA claimed that its interrogation methods enabled the United States government to find their target. Critics would say these claims amount to more dishonesty about torture, not legitimate interrogation methods. To develop this point, let's review the public discussion that followed bin Laden's death.

The White House's jubilant announcement – "We got him!" – set the tone for discussion that followed. Not only did we kill the guy, we did it with intelligence gained from enhanced interrogation techniques. Put that on your sleeve and wear it, you coddlers and bleeding hearts. Even celebration becomes a finger-pointing, I-told-you-so moment in our current political culture. When you can score points, do it.

Well, let's consider the question of time here. Apologists brag that torture is effective. You can use it to extract actionable intelligence from a prisoner. If you want to gain information about a target's current location, information you can use before the target moves, you use so-called enhanced techniques to extract information from someone who would not otherwise give it. Because these methods give you accurate, valuable, and timely data, you can use the information in your current plans.

So how was it that we used torture on our prisoners regularly to extract information, and it took us almost ten years to find Osama bin Laden? Is that what you call actionable intelligence? The braggarts might say that we merely required some time to find the right person, the key individual who had the right information. You're saying then that we torture every candidate truth-teller, until we get lucky, and find the right person? By that reasoning, you would round up every person who might know where bin Laden resides, and torture each one until you get the information you need.

Does that sound extreme? We can narrow the field quite a lot, if we focus on Pakistani intelligence officers with a need-to-know clearance for bin Laden's whereabouts. They could lead us to the man. If we round them up and strap them to a waterboard, we could probably find bin Laden in under ten years. That's a little risky, though, because what happens if you torture an intelligence officer who doesn't have the information you need?

While shilling for torture, the braggarts and apologists brought forward some intriguing story about how enhanced interrogation led us to a courier, who in turn led us to bin Laden. If the public relations people want to make such a momentous argument – that torture is justifiable because it yields the results you want – we need a story with a little more fundamental credibility. Government intelligence agencies are habitually secretive about their sources. For a mission this critical, it would never release reliable information about its intelligence gathering techniques. Or was this operation a special case, where you can reveal anything you like, including the identities of the assassins?

Unless the intelligence agencies decided to break every standard procedure they have about how they handle secret information, no one can say how the mission's planners gained their knowledge of bin Laden's location. Statements on that subject must be self-serving: convenient, unreliable PR that supports a position government adopted well before it undertook any daring operations. If the CIA wants to torture people in secret, no post-torture public relations campaign on the agency's behalf will redeem it.

Triumphalist swagger aside, you cannot justify torture under any circumstances. Even when these immoral, illegal techniques force a prisoner to reveal information, you cannot know until much later whether the information is accurate or useful. To ask an Old Testament question related to Sodom and Gomorrah, what proportion of information obtained via torture would have to be accurate and useful to justify the methods? One hundred percent? We know from much experience that no interrogation method yields information of that quality. How about seventy-five percent or fifty percent? That would mean one-quarter to one-half of the people you torture provide information that is useless.

Who but an entirely amoral person would even begin calculations like that? It reminds one of Robert McNamara's kill ratios, where he conducted nuclear warfare simulations to estimate the number of enemy combatants we have to kill to justify the innocent civilians who also die in strategic bombing raids or ballistic missile attacks. In warfare, and all enterprises that depend on cruelty, amorality amounts to immorality.

Professional interrogators recognize that torture is primitive and ineffective. You cannot tell whether the information it yields is true, or even relevant to your question. No professional interrogator will tell you that torture yields reliable information. Torture is used instead for revenge, intimidation and control. It lives in another realm, one of cruelty and brazen immorality.

People who practice this kind of cruelty are not concerned with the truth. They care about intimidation and deterrence. When Ku Klux Klan members hang a black man from a tree limb, they know what they are doing. They want retribution for a crime they have pinned on their victim, but more than that, they want a demonstration of their own power. Guilt or innocence does not actually matter that much. Hanging a person in public serves the purpose of intimidation and control quite well, whether the victim actually committed a crime or not.

Torture is like lynching, except the CIA and its affiliates do not hang their prisoners in public. They use secret military bases and prison camps. They pretend that waterboarding, sleep deprivation, solitary confinement, compliance positions, beating, and other techniques borrowed from masters of cruelty all over the world serve a legitimate, intelligence gathering purpose. Except for solitary confinement and beating, we do not routinely use these techniques within the United States, yet.

Post-9/11 torture differs from lynching in the thick layer of dishonesty we lay over the practice. Lynchers knew why they hanged people, even as they told themselves lies about their lawless administration of vigilante punishment so they could live with themselves. They executed their prisoners publicly and remorselessly to keep the people they feared impotent. Today government practices its astonishing crimes in secret, and relies on braggarts' dishonesty to legitimate what they do.

When Navy SEALs shot bin Laden twice in the head on May 2, 2011, they accomplished a task government set in our name shortly after September 11, 2001. That's the most you can say about the operation. Claims about self-defense and enhanced interrogation reflect government's habitual dishonesty about its own acts. When lies accompany a public execution of this type, you know how deeply dishonesty runs. No one, apparently, can escape its effects.

Secrecy and Security

Back when victory in the Cold War was still a prospect, in the 1980s, analysts had fixed ideas about why the conflict endured. They also held small hope the standoff would ever end, at least while they had anything to say about it. One explanation for the conflict's enduring nature was the arms race, along with the fear and edginess those large arsenals caused. Another reason was the continued occupation of Eastern Europe, which the West saw as the original cause of the conflict. A third idea was that when two great powers face each other like that, neither one will back down, for reasons of status, pride, and self-protection.

Ronald Reagan proposed an explanation of his own, one that showed his understanding of the way people and groups interact when they come into conflict. He said we could never trust the Soviet Union – as an adversary or as an ally for peace – while its government maintained a closed society. How can you have confidence in what they say, he asked, if they do everything in secret? Reagan indicated that was true not only for the Soviets' dealings internationally: the Communist party kept everything secret from its own citizens as well.

Not so long after Reagan's observation, Mikhail Gorbachev promoted glasnost – openness – as the leading edge of his initiatives for change. He apparently agreed with Reagan: no one could trust the Communist Party or the Soviet Union without openness, or transparency as we now call it. No adversaries, or potential friends, within or without the Soviet Union would make peace with its leaders, unless the leaders could create some degree of trust. Gorbachev and Reagan both grasped that trust begets goodwill. Goodwill begets peace because it helps leaders recognize where their interests coincide. Distrust fosters conflict because it is the deepest form of alienation. You can try to cooperate with someone you distrust, but the relationship does not last.

In matters of secrecy and trustworthiness, if not yet in brutality, the United States government in the twenty-first century resembles the Soviet government during the Cold War. Governments – which include intelligence agencies, internal security forces, military organizations, and regulatory bodies – have always guarded information carefully for various reasons. The United States government, however, has moved strongly away from openness and toward secrecy since 9/11. Evidence for this change is everywhere, most recently in the government's atrocious war on whistleblowers. Consequences of this change, where secrecy fosters suspicion and conflict, appear everywhere as well. Consider for instance the reactions of allied leaders who discovered the National Security Agency has been spying on them. Anger congeals into distrust when a friend betrays you.

A clear development since 2001 has been a move toward ambitious, even gigantic military and intelligence operations that require secrecy, to protect government's freedom to conduct those operations. That imperative applies abroad and at home, to warfare, torture and imprisonment, intelligence gathering and analysis, diplomacy, domestic surveillance, propaganda, threat assessment, homeland security and basic law enforcement. Practically every function of the national security state presupposes that public authorities are the sole source of information about what the state has done, is doing, or is about to do. We have no independent way to determine whether or not those authorities are honest. Therefore we have no way to know whether or not they have committed crimes.

The 9/11 attacks, themselves creatures of the national security state, destroy our democracy even now. They do so by making our government a closed organization, largely with our consent. As a result, government has alienated itself from the people it is supposed to serve. It treats citizens as enemies – people to be feared, monitored, manipulated, and controlled. In that situation, citizens skeptical of power and claims to authority naturally come to fear their government. Alienation and fear lead to obstinacy, and eventually to resistance. That is just what we find in the relationship between citizens and government in our country. We cannot trust our government when most of its acts occur in secret, when it lies to cover its crimes, and when it acts in multiple ways to conceal its motives. Secret organizations with power cannot coexist in peace with democratic institutions, or with citizens who insist upon freedom. They must be at war.

The Cold War ended when Gorbachev cracked open the Communist Party's hidden ways of power, just enough to give people some hope for honesty and happiness. An empire fell, Gorbachev lost his job, but the trust he kindled between himself and Reagan proved just enough to end a forty-five year conflict. What will happen in the antagonistic relationship between citizens and government in our country? We cannot wait two generations – half a century – to learn the answer, for tyranny once established, does not readily give way.

As we think about the issue of truth and truth telling in the context of government secrecy, we encounter another interesting connection: that between transparency and security. We associate transparency or openness with trust. Secrecy, the opposite of transparency, is more complicated. Government agencies insist secrecy is essential to protect the American people from our nation's enemies, yet the more secretive our so-called protectors become, the more insecure we feel. Friends do not need to keep secrets, only enemies, and our enemies have initials like NSA, CIA, and FBI.

In light of this basic disagreement about the purposes of secrecy, let's see why those in power regard with apprehension anyone determined to tell the truth, to reveal what must stay hidden if powerful institutions are to stay that way. Why do we think that transparency compromises security in foreign policy? If we were to conduct foreign policy openly, we would have better security as a result, not worse. By contrast, people who insist on secrecy wind up making their nations vulnerable and weak. Why? Because secrecy makes other countries distrust you, and the paths from distrust to fear, and from fear to enmity, are extraordinarily short.

People say that information is power, but the true source of power lies in transparency. That is because transparency creates trust, which is really just another form of love. No amount of coercion can ever overcome that. People who distrust you eventually hate you, whereas people who trust you become your friends. The more enemies you have, the more insecure you become. The more friends you have, the more you can rest secure. An open, reasonable foreign policy cultivates friends and minimizes enemies. Friendly relations with other countries, no matter how different they are, enhances confidence, good will, security, and safety.

A traditional realist might say, "Slow down. We don't have friends, only interests." Old school thinking says that everyone is a potential adversary. Rivalry and enmity come with competition, and the wide world is nothing if not an arena for competitive activity. Let's be realistic about the use of our power, let's understand the reasons for our success. Success comes with secrecy, because knowledge is power. When we hold key knowledge close, we will always have an advantage.

That thinking gives you officials who practice torture and fraud, aggressive wars hatched in secret, and a reputation for treachery so vivid no one would ever think to help you, let alone follow you, out of anything but fear. That kind of thinking gives you assassinations, false flag attacks, coups, and propaganda. If people can't see inside, all manner of corruption ensues. In fact, it doesn't even matter if actual corruption exists. If people can't see inside, they can't tell whether corruption exists or not. Given past behavior of power holders, people can assume safely that it does exist. Power holders do not receive benefit of the doubt here.

We come to the hardest nut in this matter of security: intelligence. The Central Intelligence Agency says it cannot disclose any information that would reveal intelligence sources and methods. That covers just about everything. With this argument, it keeps its budget secret, as well as everything else it does. Note, though, that our agencies attribute intelligence failures like 9/11 to an excess of secrecy. Whether or not you believe 9/11 occurred because of nineteen Saudi Arabians with box cutters, or for some other reason, less secrecy could have prevented it.

Openness would have exposed the plot in time. Transparent systems are self-correcting.

Increasingly, arguments that advocate secrecy apply to almost everything government does. If you request information from the feds about their activities, they have multiple reasons not to reveal the truth. They adapt arguments about the need for secrecy to any situation. Ask yourself why government would do that. A skeptic would say that it keeps information secret because it has plenty to hide. That is one reason for concealing information. No matter what the motive, when servants keep information secret from their masters, the intent is always the same: well-timed betrayal. Government officials, who are supposed to be servants, hide information for multifarious reasons. Those motives create suspicion, especially when the servants defend and justify their secret ways with still more dishonesty.

Once again, ask yourself whether government secrecy actually assures greater safety for the people government claims to protect. Here history's judgment unequivocally comes down for transparency. Secrecy hides corruption, folly, crimes, cruelty, treachery and incompetence, with no limiting power, morality, or wisdom to correct these ills. Secrecy is the hidden worm that brings down the edifice. So if you distrust the claims of government when it keeps secrets, your skepticism is well placed. If people call you unpatriotic or worse as a result, ignore the charge. You have ample history of folly committed by powerful people on your side.

Vindication of Skeptics

"The natural course of the human mind is certainly from credulity to skepticism." ~ Thomas Jefferson

George Will writes, "The strongest continuous thread in America's political tradition is skepticism about government." That means when government makes a claim, citizens respond with doubt. They routinely discount it, regard it as weakly supported, partially true, or plainly a lie. They naturally try to explain why government engages in deception so frequently, which makes them look for motives government officials may have to avoid telling the truth. This search for motives leads government's supporters to call skeptics *conspiracy theorists*.

A germane cartoon shows two stick figures in conversation. The hapless fellow on the left comments the government's official account of 9/11 is full of holes. The second guy cuts him off after eleven words, unwilling to listen, and adding insincerely that hearing the remark "breaks my heart." He urges his friend to take a second look, to be careful if you think you have uncovered a lie, because you become especially subject to confirmation bias. The more he talks, the more you see how the non-skeptic suffers from the same logical weaknesses as the people he criticizes. The conversation shows what happens when dogged self-assurance, and a pushy, almost automatic unwillingness to listen inform virtually all efforts to find the truth about important public events.

The cartoon's last frame confirms the non-skeptic's smugness. To conclude his loquacious, condescending broadside, he informs God he would like to file a bug report, to track a known glitch in human reasoning: the mind's tendency to seek confirmation of established beliefs, and to discard contradictory evidence. Yet the speaker acts immune to the bug. If confirmation bias affects everyone, though, why would it not affect our smug friend. Why would someone who asserts his position so self-confidently not point to his own arguments about conspiracy theories as an illustration of confirmation bias? Why does his reassuring litany of criticism not count? He declares with certainty that his own beliefs are true, and that opposing beliefs are "complete fictions." He seems just as sure of himself as the people he mocks.

Most notably, he does not pause to consider evidence, or listen to his friend's reasoning. He cuts his friend off, sure that whatever he wants to say about 9/11 is nonsense. How does he know arguments that challenge the official version of events on 9/11 are insupportable? He doesn't say. He merely belittles other people's beliefs. On this flimsy foundation, he simpers that his heart breaks because his friend cannot distinguish between what is true and what is false. He dismisses all arguments he labels conspiracy theories – throws them into the same discard pile. Why bother to look at evidence for each one, if they all fit the same pattern? When you've heard one, you've heard them all. They all come from the same source: that "known glitch in human reasoning." They all result in false beliefs.

Here is a closing point about rhetorical requirements for presentation of evidence. When you make an argument, do not cherry pick your examples. Cherry pickers select only those examples that support their main points, and ignore other obvious examples that do not – exactly what you do not want to do if your main point is about the dangers of confirmation bias. If you do not believe alternate accounts of 9/11, your obvious touchstone for comparison is Kennedy's assassination and the Warren Commission report. Both 9/11 and Kennedy's murder are notorious crimes followed by doubtful official reports. Yet the closest we come to anything having to do with the government in the cartoon is a controversy over the moon landing – a disagreement about propaganda and public relations, not about criminal activity.

Conspiracy theorists regard themselves as skeptics. They see people who accept mainstream or official accounts as credulous. A mirror image holds for people who reject conspiracy theories. Equally skeptical and equally self-assured, this group regards conspiracy theorists as credulous. Each side regards the other as too willing to accept false or questionable information.

Interestingly, conspiracy theorists tend to be more conservative in the terms they choose to describe their antagonists. On the other side, defenders of official accounts may use terms like *whacko, beyond crazy,* or *nut job* when they refer to conspiracy theorists. When you hear those phrases, take a moment to think why a person would use words like that. Why is ridicule their first response. If contradictory evidence underlies the disagreement, think about motives that might make someone call another person insane. Consider whether people who comfortably dismiss others with terms of ridicule and ostracism have grounded their beliefs on different types of evidence, or responded with a balanced, discerning treatment of skeptics' questions. People who value deliberation and analysis generally do not use words like that.

Historically, remember this important point when you hear people ridicule conspiracy theorists: independent researchers were right about the Kennedy assassination. Not every theory about who shot Kennedy, or why he was shot, is correct, but skeptics were correct to say that the government's investigation was incomplete, that the case was not closed. After so many people dismissed independent researchers who began their work as skeptics, the outcome of their research vindicated both their tenacity, and their desire to comprehend all of the evidence related to the case.

That does not mean all conspiracy theories are correct. It does mean that we should never give benefit of doubt to official accounts. Official accounts necessarily displace responsibility – away from officials. Officials have not earned trust, do not deserve it, and certainly do not need it. The initial presumption for all investigations should be that the federal government is not trustworthy, that it does not tell the truth, and that anything it says in a particular instance is unreliable. Why would it even trouble itself with an investigation and written report if it did not need to allay well grounded doubts about its reliability? It has no claim on our beliefs.

If that seems overly skeptical, ask which is more reasonable, or safe, when stakes are high: to disbelieve institutions of proven dishonesty, or to grant them a third or a fourth chance. You might give a family member a second chance after a relatively minor instance of dishonesty, but is it reasonable to give governmental institutions – in particular intelligence and investigative agencies – a second chance after their demonstrable involvement in something as grave as the murder of a president? The wise course is to distrust a government like that, ignore it, set it aside, and create one in its place that does not harbor secrets about crimes it has committed.

The fitness of dishonest governments – the question of whether they have any claim at all on our loyalty – burdens discussion of conspiracy theories with more weight than most conversations can bear. Skeptics may act rather matter-of-fact about their beliefs, where for many, departure from orthodox beliefs may appear calamitous. Some fear the heavens may actually fall. Yet to discount conspiracy theories because they threaten a stable worldview certainly endangers everyone far more than discovery of the truth. To place your faith in a government that is actually an enemy clearly places you in a more dangerous position than any other civic mistake you might make.

Thoroughgoing skepticism of every official pronouncement – from everyday spin and self-serving arguments to formal investigative reports – gives citizens a robust strategy for safety and freedom, if they can bear the discomfort or sense of exclusion they may experience if they do not participate in mainstream arguments. Automatically denying authority or credibility to everything government says may seem to entail extraordinary cognitive overhead, but in fact it makes sorting information more efficient. When you disbelieve anything that originates with government, especially when the statement is consequential, you have a practical and accurate filter to sort evidence and discern truth.

As we evaluate skepticism and attitudes associated with it, we should also remember the value of a Zen-like detachment from the world of argumentation and political alignments. Skeptical viewpoints become hard to maintain in the swirling currents of partisanship. When people speak on behalf of government, or analysts align themselves with a mainstream version of events, be slow to judge and open to all possibilities in your response. Above all, be cautious about reaching any conclusions until you have considered important pieces of evidence yourself. In the end no one cares which side you take, except you. No one cares whether you take any side at all.

The real world of political discourse, however, is anything but Zen-like. Michael Moynihan concludes, in a *Daily Beast* article about reactions to the Newtown mass casualty exercise, that conspiracy theorists are not people he cares to associate with: "After a week among the anti-Zionist conspiracy theorists, the pop-eyed Infowarriors, and various autodidacts and 'independent researchers,' I'm convinced that America is indeed overflowing with people who need their heads checked out."

I think of autodidacts and independent researchers – no quotation marks here – as people who think for themselves. Apparently Moynihan, and our cartoon's protagonist, regard them as mildly insane, delusional, worthy only of disdain and dismissal. Moynihan does not say straight out that pop-eyed Infowarriors pose a danger to the rest of us, but you still wonder why he would choose a word like *pop-eyed*. When you regard people who disagree with you as insane, you have stepped into uneasy territory. The landscape looks strange when you are not with your friends, its atmosphere somewhat threatening. Then you remember how much conflict and estrangement among groups turns on divergent beliefs, rather than greed or a primitive instinct for domination. You can transform other people into fearsome threats – objects, actually – merely because they do not think the same way you do. That's something to be skeptical about.

Afterword:

Responses to Political Iniquity

I've said it so many times, in so many places: "If the feds torture people in public, what do that do in secret?" Plenty, it turns out: consider MK-ULTRA. The feds aren't "doing" MK-ULTRA now, you say. The program ended a long time ago. I don't see the chronology of crime quite that way. If someone commits a crime in secret a long time ago, and keeps the crime a secret in the present, the crime has not ended. It may be suspended, in effect, but it has not ended.

Falsehood before becomes falsehood forever, or at least indefinitely, until truth emerges. A poisonous lie pollutes everything downstream: culture, human ties, legitimate authority, faith and trust, certainly sincerity. Dishonesty becomes a way of life, as nothing survives the absence of truth, any more than vegetation survives the absence of water. That is why people attuned to society's needs urge truth first, then reconciliation after people have wronged each other in major ways. We heard this message about how to heal in Lincoln's Second Inaugural Address, as the Civil War neared its end.

I mentioned MK-ULTRA briefly – if you learn even a little about this program, you will understand why I raise it in this context. Its history indicates what happens when truth does not emerge, when crimes go not only unpunished, but largely unknown, except by their perpetrators and their victims. The lethal poison unlocked by this type of unacknowledged crime never leaves the social body.

Let me mention one other case, the Dreyfus Affair, where people spent years to force the truth into the open. In that way, the Affair is similar to investigations about Kennedy's murder and the 9/11 attacks. Many who resisted truth about political crimes in America used exactly the same reasons and strategies 120 years ago, in France, to convince others that it's best to leave these crimes alone. Don't expose the truth, when truth threatens to destroy everything you respect, to overturn your faith in other people. Significantly, advocates for truth in both eras used similar arguments as well: if we do not acknowledge what happened, we are done as a society. Our efforts to live together will fail.

Essays like these can tell you a lot, in a short space, about differing points of view. That is especially true for contested issues like the Kennedy assassination and 9/11. Students of both episodes in our history know the arguments associated with each. These are controversial issues not only because crimes can be inherently difficult to solve, but also because they involve fundamental understandings about our government, and our country. Moreover, arguments about them play out in a turbulent social and political environment. These arguments are not parlor games. The conclusions we reach affect how we define our membership in the American community, or whether a real community as we conceive it even exists.

9/11 occurred about thirty-eight years after Kennedy's assassination. The social and political environment in the United States changed a great deal during that time. One thing did not change: if you disagree with the government's account of what happened on November 22, 1963, or September 11, 2001, you will encounter ridicule, mocking attacks, and rude contempt. 9/11 researchers observed what happened to Kennedy researchers. They saw the Kennedy researchers prevail nevertheless, after nearly fifty years of work. 9/11 researchers understand that we may not have fifty years to solve this case. If the truth about 9/11 waits until 2051, we may not see any remnants of the American republic left. In fact, hardly any exist now.

Based on the way successful 9/11 researchers undertake their work, we can identify a few best practices. Researchers want their work and the language they use to persuade people, or at least to provoke second thoughts. Few want to work carefully, in good faith, only to hear ridicule and contempt. Given the nature of these crimes, researchers can expect strong, negative reactions when they imply state complicity. Yet one hopes to build a body of work that gains a hearing among some thoughtful people, who take time to follow a line of reasoning, and who constrain their judgment until they comprehend that reasoning. One hopes to build a persuasive body of work, no matter how long it takes. Yet given what is at stake, time does matter.

These practices emerge as one compares the work researchers have done on 9/11, with experience researchers have gained during decades since Kennedy's assassination.

Develop a common vocabulary and mode of argument

Develop a rich language that frames the agenda for discussion. The language should not be arcane or antagonistic, but should encourage people to join the conversation. The language should begin with general arguments, and lead to more detailed ones. It should start with the big picture, and move from there to stories about people involved with the crime.

A simple example is use of the word conspiracy. It's meaning is simple – more than one person involved in planning or executing a crime – but the word became an epithet in debates about Kennedy's death. Conspiracy theorists became conspiracy buffs, who became conspiracy nuts. That evolution of the phrase well serves apologists for the Warren Commission, but it does not help you find the truth. Truth likes language a little more impartial than that.

A key difference for 9/11 research is that everyone agrees from the start that the crime was a conspiracy. A lone actor did not destroy the twin towers. The question becomes, which actors? 9/11 researchers recognize that opponents cannot use the word conspiracy against them, as opponents did in the Kennedy case. Of course, that hasn't prevented opponents from brandishing the label conspiracy theorist anyway. 9/11 researchers have insisted that conspiracy is a neutral term in this debate – our task is to determine which conspiracy.

Let's consider one more label briefly. How did truther become a term of derision? When Stephen Colbert, a comedian and satirist, uses the word truthiness, that's useful to him in making people laugh and think. Politics operates without satire. When truther comes into widespread use as a put-down for people who say, let's take another look, you know you have entered an Orwellian environment of newspeak, where ironic double meanings induce you to join the club of right thinking folks. The very concept of truth becomes a tool of derision for propagandists.

Show courtesy, respect, and self-confidence

Treat opponents better than they treat you. Courtesy and respect communicate self-confidence. These qualities help you stay positive about inevitable ridicule. They help you feel comfortable with your arguments. They save you from seeing the other side force you to play defense. You want to control the ball. Respectful and courteous methods of argument, backed by self-confidence, help you do that.

A double standard usually reveals that something is not right in the bigger picture. One side freely uses words like whacko, nut case, wingnut, conspiracy buff, truther (apparently reserved for 9/11 skeptics), and others. These terms are clearly derogatory, and evidence-free. That is, they displace reasoned argument. Once you begin by calling your adversary a whacko, you don't need to bother with an argument at all. In fact, arguing with a whacko makes you look bad. Once you start with the epithets, you don't need to say anything reasonable.

One waits – a long time – to hear someone say, "Wait a minute, that kind of name calling isn't so helpful here." It takes you back to elementary school, doesn't it? Now imagine the response if skeptics routinely relied on name calling to address people who disagree with them. Let's say, out of the gate, researchers into Kennedy's murder accused people who believe Oswald did it of being whackos. Would you encounter the same nonchalant silence in that case? To the contrary, non-skeptics would say that the impolite vocabulary confirms their negative assessment of the skeptics' sanity.

Occasionally you read a book review where a skeptic says you have to be an idiot to believe the official story, whether it's about JFK or 9/11. It's kind of satisfying, after all the abuse, to see a strong word thrown back. For the moment, it feels good to be on the offensive, working as part of a team that feels confident enough to use a word like that. Satisfying though it might be, the costs of giving in to reciprocal name calling are pretty high. Continue to treat your opponents with courtesy and respect. Set an example of politeness, and insist on respect in return. Eventually people will perceive the obvious double standard that applies to arguments from each side. You cannot ignore a disparity that wide for too long.

Focus on persuasive, key evidence

For the Kennedy assassination, government agencies from the Dallas police to the Federal Bureau of Investigation effectively destroyed, dismissed, ignored, or tampered with a lot of evidence. They cleaned up, tore apart, and rebuilt Kennedy's limousine as quickly as possible. They performed an incompetent and, one might say, criminal autopsy on Kennedy's body. They permitted Lee Oswald's murder. Johnson formed an investigative commission led by people like Allen Dulles, one of Kennedy's most vigorous and motivated enemies. The investigative commission relied on evidence assembled by the FBI under J. Edgar Hoover, another of JFK's enemies.

As a result, it took time for Kennedy researchers to reach an appreciable level of agreement about key evidence. Everyone recognized the importance of Abraham Zapruder's film, but for a number of reasons, interpretation of that film led to an amazing amount of disagreement. Combined with other evidence, such as where pieces of Kennedy's brain landed after his head blew apart, the film demonstrates that the Warren Commission was wrong. The film was not released until twelve years after Kennedy's murder, however, so the overall trail of evidence was well cold by then.

Government pursued similar tactics for the 9/11 investigation, except the president resisted formation of any commission at all. The number of victims was large, and so was the pressure, so Bush eventually relented, and formed the 9/11 Commission to determine what happened that day. Like the Warren Commission, it started with a set of conclusions, and evaluated evidence in light of its destination. Unsurprisingly, given its methods, its work was just as poor as the Warren Commission's. Moreover, many people received its findings with a similar level of skepticism. "Really?" they said. "That's what you found?" The Bush administration knew that was a likely reaction. That's why it resisted formation of the commission to begin with. Why commission all that work if you know the results will be false, and transparently false?

Now we arrive at questions about key evidence in the 9/11 case. The event that most persuasively points to 9/11 as a false flag operation is the collapse of World Trade Center building number seven near the end of the day, about eight and a half hours after the initial attacks. The collapse of this building in free fall was a controlled demolition, not the result of contained fires that burned inside the building during the day. The collapse of this building in free fall looked exactly like the collapse of other large, steel-framed buildings brought down in the same way. When you try to understand why WTC7 fell as it did, when it did, you encounter a chain of questions that leads you from one disturbing conclusion to the next.

9/11 researchers correctly regard the collapse of WTC7 as their starting point. Like Jack Ruby's hit of Lee Oswald two days after JFK's murder, the collapse of WTC7 shortly before dusk on September 11 reveals too much to be ignored. After you digest the significance of these two critical events, everything about government's explanation of the larger crimes feels artificial and false.

Stress scientific reasoning

Scientific reasoning starts with how one collects and evaluates evidence, and reaches well beyond that. When applied to forensic analysis, it requires you to work backward from fragmented, hard-to-find evidence, under uncertain hypotheses, to reconstruct an event that you can never reproduce, or verify first-hand. Forensic analysis requires the skills of Holmes, not so much the skills of Watson and Crick.

We are used to reasoning forward from premises, what-if questions, thought experiments, laboratory trials, carefully recorded data, trial and error, observations, tests, and comparisons. When you apply these methods to solution of a crime, you must adapt them to an environment where you cannot conduct experiments as such. Instead, you must try to reconstruct the big bang from evidence scattered throughout the universe.

Two pieces of analysis about the Kennedy assassination illustrate these points. Watch a YouTube video of Vincent Bugliosi, where he discusses the work of researchers who disagree with him. As he defends his work, he can run other people down, or he can use evidence from his own research to demonstrate that his conclusions are superior. From these interviews, Bugliosi appears to be a smart man who does not have much to say. His laces his sentences with words like idiotic, wrong-headed, and misguided to describe those who present evidence that counters his own. Consequently he spends practically no time discussing his evidence! Contrast that with Bob Harris's treatment of the same event and the same evidence. When you have watched Harris's presentation, you know you have seen forensic analysis that makes effective use of scientific reasoning.

We all know how to reason scientifically. We all recognize valid scientific reasoning when we encounter it. Teachers often illustrate it with simple examples. It requires practice to apply the same methods to more complex cases. In every instance, scientific reasoning asks you to test hypotheses against evidence. You use hypotheses to help you decide which evidence is germane, and which is not. You try to reach reasonable conclusions based on evidence you have available. You try not to reach beyond the evidence, but you make the best use of evidence you have. If you speculate or make educated guesses, you distinguish those from your conclusions. Again, watch Bob Harris to see a master at work.

9/11 researchers are correct to rely on scientific arguments when they analyze evidence related to the 9/11 attacks. Critics of 9/11 research, like Vincent Bugliosi in Kennedy's case, will call 9/11 researchers idiots and nuts to denigrate both their evidence and their conclusions. Set against valid analysis, these names appear pretty small. Bob Harris sets a standard of analysis that no defender of the Warren report, including xxx Posner in Case Closed, has matched. The quality of Harris's analysis speaks for itself. The quality of analysis in the Warren report and the 9/11 Commission report speaks for itself, too.

The quality of your analysis serves as the best bulwark against ridicule.

Promote collaboration

To see the importance of moral support and collective endeavor, consider the attacks on Jim Garrison, the courageous New Orleans district attorney who, in a suit against Clay Shaw, marshaled evidence of government complicity in Kennedy's murder. He dealt with infiltrators, witness tampering, hostile press coverage, overt and implicit threats, and all kinds of contempt and ridicule. Washington's tactics to discredit and frustrate Garrison came to define the idea and practical use of dirty tricks for the 1960s. Yet his work endured over decades, and his conclusions proved correct.

What would have happened if his backers during the 1960s had been able to speak with a firmer, more unified voice? Would the history of research into the Kennedy assassination have changed? We don't know the answer to that, but we do know that efforts to disprove the Warren Commission's conclusions during the 1960s met furious resistance from several quarters. Lacking effective means of cooperation, people who agreed with Garrison had to wait a long time to see his efforts validated.

9/11 researchers can communicate more effectively, but the resistance is just as stout. Moreover, the Internet can promote isolation and distrust, just as easily as it can promote community and collaboration based on trust. Cass Sunstein, administrator of the aptly named Office of Information and Regulatory Affairs, advocates openly that government infiltrate communities of 9/11 researchers to sow disagreement, spread falsehood and suspicion, and use these techniques to break them up.

Propagandists call these methods cognitive infiltration. Open advocacy of such turpitude shows contempt for your opponents – doesn't it? – not to mention contempt for the government you represent. You declare that your opponents are too weak and inept to counter you, even if they know what you want to do. Worse still, it shows you expect people, the citizens you serve, to back you in such an immoral plan.

Sunstein argues that these measures are necessary and justified because the 9/11 truth movement is corrosive, without considering the effects of his own cynicism. We have witnessed evidently cynical propaganda techniques, worldwide, for a long time now. Sunstein's proposals unmistakably show how government self-interest actively undermines good-faith efforts to find the truth.

If Cass Sunstein followed David Ray Griffin's argumentative approach, he would meet 9/11 researchers on level ground, to fight them point by point. He would not talk about devious, dastardly government tactics that confirm nearly every point 9/11 researchers make. Honest, courageous people like Griffin charge Sunstein's government with complicity in a monstrous crime designed to sow fear, panic and division among the citizenry. What government official, responsible for upholding free speech and free information, would want to use invidious, divisive falsehoods to break up groups that support Griffin, in order to counter a charge like that?

Sunstein cannot have it both ways. Either members of the 9/11 truth movement have important things to say, in which case members of a complicit government do in fact have something to fear. Or, members of the 9/11 truth movement believe in Santa Claus fantasies and falsehoods, in which case they are harmless. Sunstein dismisses the movement's beliefs as fantasies, yet advocates a large government program to destroy their credibility and cooperation. At bottom, Sunstein recognizes the extreme danger to government if the 9/11 truth movement can unite and collaborate effectively. Absent anticipated danger, cognitive infiltration becomes beside the point. Any strategist will say: deploy your resources economically, and only where required.

Having mentioned a moral man like David Ray Griffin, let me make one more remark about how communities based on truth form. It also counts as a warning to governments who underestimate their opponents: watch out for theologians and other leaders who care about truth! They will bring you down. They unite people because they believe freedom and truth always defeat criminal, cynical behavior. They care about what is right. We can remember religious leaders like Martin Luther, and move straight to heroes like Mahatma Gandhi, Jack Kennedy, Martin Luther King, Bobby Kennedy, Karol Wojtyla, Lech Walesa, Nelson Mandela, Liu Xiaobo, Aung San Suu Kyi, Bradley Manning, Edward Snowden, and less known leaders everywhere who currently struggle to achieve freedom and dignity for others. If you go up against people like these, you will eventually lose – even if the struggle requires decades, and you destroy a lot of people in your defeat.

Patience yields persuasive results

Let the researchers and writers involved in this search for truth, let anyone who wants to learn the truth to preserve our republic, think of stories we can tell. If we quote witnesses, the witnesses ought to have names. If we know of incriminating evidence found in the towers' remains, listeners want to know who found the evidence, what they did with it, and who analyzed it. Listeners want to identify with real people who interact with other real people, and who do things. Why do you suppose the government did not reveal the life stories of the people who attacked us on 9/11? It did not do so because it has too much to hide. It could not personalize the attackers' stories without revealing information that it would prefer to keep hidden.

Stories about actual people lead to reasoning about motives and actions tied to those motives. Early Kennedy researchers focused, among other things, on the Warren Report and its weaknesses, medical reports, forensic evidence and its interpretations, as well as basic facts gleaned from photographs and eye witness interviews. That was necessary preparative work, but it did not become truly persuasive until researchers attributed motives to the actors. We might think of the possibility that Kennedy's assassination was a coup d'état, but such ideas remain unpersuasive if conspirators have murky motives for murdering a president. In books like James Douglass's *JFK and the Unspeakable*, we could see at last why Kennedy's killers wanted him to die. Douglass tells a complicated story to reveal those motives.

The same narrative methods have already started to drive 9/11 research. Which is more persuasive, to say that tiny chips indicative of nano-thermite were found in the towers' dust, or to relate details about who discovered it, and what happened after that? Above those details, researchers like David Ray Griffin connect events in Manhattan with initiation of war in Baghdad eighteen months later. Effective researchers tell a story, the way an attorney tells a story in front of a jury. If we don't have enough good accounts now, find people who were present that day and ask them to write down everything they remember. Banish the passive voice from investigative reports. Replace it with a narrative that explains who acted, when they acted, what they did, and why.

We can still find out what happened that day. We used to think that the more time passed after November 22, 1963, the more difficult it would be to learn the truth about Kennedy's assassination. If anything, books about the assassination during the last ten years have been as rich and detailed as you could ask.

Evidently we needed the Kennedy research pot to simmer for a long time. Patience yields persuasive results.

9/11 research does not have such a long time to simmer. Fifty years ago, conspirators killed our president. We let them get away with it. Thirty-seven and a half years later, another calamity struck in lower Manhattan. We let the conspirators get away with it again. When U. S. armed forces tipped bin Laden's weighted body overboard and let it sink to the bottom of the ocean, we did not reach the end of this story. When we assassinated Osama bin Laden, we did not complete our responsibility to our republic, to 9/11 victims or their family members, or to ourselves as citizens. Before we do that, we want to know what actually happened on September 11, 2001.

Looking ahead

These practices concern language or rhetoric of debate. Persuasion occurs via verbal and social means. Naturally people who engage in persuasion pay attention to language, and to means of communication. The huge difference between 1963 and 2001 is that the Internet did not exist in 1963. We had Walter Cronkite and the local newspaper. Go on YouTube to watch television news coverage from the afternoon of November 22. You witness a different era in communications, without a doubt.

Kennedy researchers in the years after 1963 operated at a big disadvantage by comparison with 9/11 researchers. Government could control the narrative and dissemination of evidence more surely than they can now. In fact, research on the Kennedy assassination, and reassessment of its conclusions, developed during the twenty years after Oliver Stone's film, *JFK*, in the early 1990s. That period coincides with the development of new methods of communication, including the Internet.

Government possesses several key advantages in the debate over what happened on 9/11. It also operates with some disadvantages. It recognizes that if it cannot control communications channels, and thereby break up communities, it will lose in the end. That is why it works so hard to regain the kind of control it had in the 1960s. We have some confidence that, eventually, government's efforts to control key communications channels will fail. We can expect that, eventually, officials' efforts to disrupt collaboration may not yield the results they seek. Less certain is whether 9/11 researchers can overcome disadvantages on their side. Today's researchers need discipline, and faith their work has prospects of success. If *we* remain mindful of what we – investigators and non-investigators alike – have all learned since 1963, we may see an opportunity, soon, to make a reasoned case in a less hostile, more open atmosphere.

About the Author

Steven Greffenius graduated from Reed College with a degree in history, and later from the University of Iowa with a Ph.D. in political science. In between he served as electronics material officer aboard USS KIRK (FF-1087) in the Western Pacific.

Currently, Steve lives with his family in Westwood, Massachusetts, outside of Boston. He founded *The Jeffersonian* to publish essays on political ethics, democracy and public affairs. Visit sgreffenius.com for resources related to this and other books about politics.

www.ingramcontent.com/pod-product-compliance
Lightning Source LLC
Chambersburg PA
CBHW020513290526
45786CB00002B/582